HAUNTED GROUND

GHOST STORIES FROM THE ROCK

HAUNTED GROUND

GHOST STORIES FROM THE ROCK

D A L E   J A R V I S

FLANKER PRESS LIMITED
ST. JOHN'S

Library and Archives Canada Cataloguing in Publication

Jarvis, Dale, 1971-, author
Haunted Ground : ghost stories from the Rock
/ Dale Jarvis.

Includes index.
Issued in print and electronic formats.
ISBN 978-1-77117-622-4 (paperback).--ISBN 978-1-77117-623-1
(epub).--ISBN 978-1-77117-624-8 (kindle).--ISBN 978-1-77117-625-5 (pdf)

A CIP catalogue record for this book is available from Library and Archives Canada.

PRINTED IN CANADA

MIX
Paper from responsible sources
FSC® C016245
www.fsc.org

This paper has been certified to meet the environmental and social standards of the Forest Stewardship Council® (FSC®) and comes from responsibly managed forests, and verified recycled sources.

Cover Design by Graham Blair

FLANKER PRESS LTD.
PO BOX 2522, STATION C
ST. JOHN'S, NL
CANADA

TELEPHONE: (709) 739-4477 FAX: (709) 739-4420 TOLL-FREE: 1-866-739-4420
WWW.FLANKERPRESS.COM

9 8 7 6 5 4 3

Canada
Canada Council for the Arts Conseil des Arts du Canada
Newfoundland Labrador

We acknowledge the [financial] support of the Government of Canada. *Nous reconnaissons l'appui [financier] du gouvernement du Canada*. We acknowledge the support of the Canada Council for the Arts, which last year invested $153 million to bring the arts to Canadians throughout the country. *Nous remercions le Conseil des arts du Canada de son soutien. L'an dernier, le Conseil a investi 153 millions de dollars pour mettre de l'art dans la vie des Canadiennes et des Canadiens de tout le pays*. We acknowledge the financial support of the Government of Newfoundland and Labrador, Department of Tourism, Culture and Recreation for our publishing activities..

CONTENTS

ACKNOWLEDGEMENTS.......... ix

INTRODUCTION.......... xi

CHAPTER ONE: TOKENS, PREMONITIONS, AND THE GREAT BEYOND

The Wiltshire Token
Port Union.......... 3

Voices on the Labrador
Red Bay and Emily Harbour.......... 7

Poor Joe Benoit
Garia Bay.......... 13

The Premonition of the *Southern Cross*
Trinity and Birchy Cove, Trinity Bay.......... 19

A Smell of Death
Spaniard's Bay and Carbonear.......... 23

Saying Farewell
Islington.......... 29

One for Sorrow
Marystown, Spaniard's Bay, Bay Roberts, South River, Cape la Hune, and Doctor's Harbour.......... 33

CHAPTER TWO: SHADES OF YESTERYEAR

Ferries and Phantom Ferrymen
Bell Island, St. John's, and Trinity, Trinity Bay.......... 47

Mrs. King's House
Boyd's Cove.....49
The Ghost of Mrs. Pride
Pilley's Island.....51
The Mortuary Wreath
Crouse.....55
The Legend of Kitty Casey
Elliston.....59
Astride a Pale Horse
Mount Pearl, Mattis Point, and Bay Roberts.....63

CHAPTER THREE: HISTORICAL AND CONTEMPORARY LEGENDS

Lights in the Fog
Nain, Tors Cove, Head of Bay D'Espoir, Harbour Breton, and Sandy Cove.....69
The Haunted Trestle Revisited
Clarke's Beach.....77
Hark! Phantom Drummers and Pipers
Marysvale, Brigus, Bay Roberts, and Swift Current.....83
Mysterious Norsemen
L'Anse aux Meadows, Bay de L'Eau, Harbour Mille, and Muddy Cove.....95
Red Eyes and Rod Stewart
Glovertown.....105
The Webber
Western Newfoundland.....115

CHAPTER FOUR: LOCATIONS OF MYSTERY

Buried Treasure and Ghostly Guardians
Clarke's Beach, Bay Roberts, Port de Grave, Torbay, Musgrave Harbour, Bonavista, Shoal Bay, and Money Point.......131
Father Duffy's Well
Salmonier Line.......139
Fogo Island's Many Spirits
Fogo Island.......147
Those Bloody Rocks
Tilting, Alexander Bay, New Perlican, Hant's Harbour, and Red Indian Lake.......155
The Boulevard's Black and White Ghost
St. John's.......161

CHAPTER FIVE: DARKNESS AND THE LIGHT

The Devil at the Dance
Brigus and Spaniard's Bay.......169
Reading the Cards
Joe Batt's Arm.......173
Wicked Witches
St. John's, Joe Batt's Arm, Comfort Cove, and Colliers.......177
The Cat Who Wasn't There
St. John's and Carbonear.......187
Heavenly Representatives
Carbonear, Bonavista, and Heart's Content.......193
Bedtime with the Old Hag
Coming soon to a mattress near you.......197

WORKS REFERENCED 207

INDEX 215

ACKNOWLEDGEMENTS

A great number of people have helped in the production of this book. Thank you to everyone who pointed me to sources, told me stories, read drafts, and helped me track down more information:

Ryan Adams, Garland Bailey, Rhoda Bailey, Dean Barnes, W. Ritchie Benedict, John Bodner, Erin Boyd, Bruce Brenton, Emma Burry, Ashley Byrne, Eanie Clarke, Marilyn Coles-Hayley, Brittany Corbett, Maggie Courish, Ron Delaney, Gail de Vos, Norma Dollimount, Jenelle Duval, Cynthia Egan, Heather Elliott, Holly Everett, Anne Farrell, Paula Feltham, Chantel Fisher, Mike Flynn, Francis Furlong, Bill Gilbert, Wesley Gosse, Shannon Green, Christine Hennebury, Denise Hennebury, Philip Hiscock, Anastacia Hopkins, Sherry House, Matthew Howse, John Nick Jeddore, Allan Jøn, George Jones, Kelly Jones, Jeff Keeping, Danielle Larmon, Christa Marshall, Pauline Chislett Masters, Eileen Balsom Matthews, Alice Moores, Rebekah Nolan, Gina Noordhof, Angela Noseworthy, Travis George Parsons, Dee Payne, Cindy Pearson, Daniel Penney, June Penney, Barry Penton, Dean Penton, Lloyd Pike, Bride Power, Tony Power, Molly Quinn, Kate Rideout, Sandra Roach, Debbie Robbins, Paula

Roberts, Josh Russell, Shirley Ryan, Kharis Samms, Grace Shears, Lynette Snook, Megan Somerton, Dave Sullivan, Victoria Swyers, Alan Taylor, Dwayne Tuck, Grant Tucker, Krista Wall, Kimberley Welsh, Doug Wells, Rhonda Whalen, Lisa Wilson, Harry and Elizabeth Young.

Thanks as well to those who shared stories but preferred some anonymity: Becky, Brandon, Caitlin, Carolyn, Cindy, Jeff, Julia, Kerri, Krista, Kristin, Louise, Mary, Nadine, Nicole, Ryan, Sandy, Sara, Sheila, Sheldon, Susan, and Tara.

INTRODUCTION

Searchers for pirate gold may still be held in thrall by legends that linger in Newfoundland. Phantom ships and ghostly lights still presage storm, and fairies dance in grassy dells on moonlit nights. Here in our land history speaks through age-old ballads, ancient custom, and quaint dialects.

— L. E. F. English, *Newfoundland Quarterly*, 1949

The briefly named Short Beach runs between Coley's Point, Bay Roberts, and Bareneed. Many years ago there was a terrible storm in Conception Bay, and in the wind, rain, and darkness, a schooner ran aground on Short Beach and was dashed to pieces by fearsome waves. All hands were lost, and it is believed that the only survivor of the wreck was a dog.

On stormy nights in Coley's Point, a great black hound emerges out of the ocean, dripping wet. It pads up and down over the rocks, howling mournfully in the rain from one end of Short Beach to the other, a supernatural witness to one of Newfoundland and Labrador's countless shipwrecks.

Or so the legend goes.

Every stretch of coastline in the province has a shipwreck story, and many of those have ghostly reminders of those tragedies. Some, like the black dog of Coley's Point, occur when conditions match the time of the wreck. Some ghost ships appear to warn of coming bad weather, while others reappear on the anniversary of the wreck itself.

Not every community has a ghostly shipwreck story, but every community has its own folklore and intangible heritage.

Yet there is an omnipresent danger in our communities of these stories being lost. We look to our glowing screens and we hungrily devour stories that come from away, while the tales that nourished the imagination of previous generations are sometimes passed over in search of more exotic fare. We are rich in stories here in Newfoundland and Labrador, and we need to ensure that our folklore and our oral history is passed from one generation to the next.

This collection of ghostly tales is, in a small way, part of that transmission of cultural knowledge. Some of the stories in this book are old, some are new. Some are personal accounts of true hauntings, some are urban or contemporary legends, and some are tales of special places steeped in local folklore. Here, you will meet intriguing characters from Newfoundland and Labrador's past and present and delve into the lore and legends behind some of our myths, folk beliefs, and fears.

Enjoy the stories! And, as always, if you have one of your own to share, I would love to hear it.

Dale Jarvis
@dalejarvis
dale@dalejarvis.ca
www.hauntedhike.com

CHAPTER ONE

Tokens, Premonitions, and the Great Beyond

An old fisherman, who shall be nameless, takes his cranky little boat along to the fishing grounds, now he finds himself in the water, the boat has gone down neath his feet, and the relentless sea has claimed yet another victim. His daughter at home is grief-stricken, yet not entirely unprepared for the terrible stroke.

Why? Because just a few days before his "Token" had walked into the bedroom fully clad in oil clothes, and sou'wester, and sat down by the side the bed. At the time this happened the man was at his nets and did not return until hours later.

— Charles Jamieson, *Newfoundland Quarterly*, December 1928

THE WILTSHIRE TOKEN

Port Union

In 2014, I got an intriguing email from Chantel Fisher, who was then a seventeen-year-old ghost story enthusiast from Bonavista. Fisher had spent the past summer working at the Heritage Shop in Bonavista and had been reading one of my previous books on Newfoundland ghost stories, *Haunted Waters.*

"I notice you have many stories about St. John's and I would like to see some smaller towns' stories in your book," she wrote. "My family has always loved sharing ghost stories and have shared some with me."

Fisher then went on to retell one of her favourite family stories, one she had learned from her grandfather. The story is of one of the most common types of stories I hear from Newfoundlanders—a token story.

A token is where someone has some sort of supernatural warning or premonition that someone close to them is about to die or has just died. In many cases, these stories are quite touching and show the strong emotional ties between relatives. For the most part, these are not evil or angry ghosts, just people who want a chance to say farewell. Rarely are they as dramatic as what happened to Fisher's grandfather.

Anguish. Illustration by Tony Johannot, 1838.

"My pop's name was Wesley Wiltshire," Fisher told me. "He's the one who told me the story."

The story took place in the early 1900s, in Port Union,

and involved Fisher's great-grandfather, Ezra Wiltshire.

"My pop passed away several years ago now," says Fisher, "but my great-grandfather's token still remains in my mind. My great-grandfather had a very sick brother who lived with them and slept in their spare bedroom downstairs. He had pneumonia and was too sick to even get up out of bed. One night my great-grandfather checked on his brother and gave him some water before he went to bed."

Fisher's grandfather told her, "Father said that his brother was the same as always and he didn't think that he'd last much longer."

Later that night, Fisher's great-grandfather and his wife were upstairs in bed, asleep. The husband woke up to the sound of his bedroom door slamming, and he looked up to see his brother, standing at the foot of the bed.

"Brother?" said the man. "What are you doing here?"

At this, the brother took hold of the foot of the bed and started shaking the frame with such force that the occupants were almost flung from it.

"Father didn't know what to think," Fisher's grandfather told her. "He knew his brother was too sick to climb the stairs, let alone take hold of the bed and almost flip them over."

When Ezra Wiltshire looked again, his brother had vanished. He looked over at his wife, who had slept on, un-

Ezra Wiltshire, 1945. Photo courtesy Sir William F. Coaker Heritage Foundation, Port Union.

disturbed by the commotion, a fact which confused him further.

"He jumped from the bed and ran downstairs to his brother's room," describes Fisher. "When he opened the door, the glass of water was tipped over and his brother was dead in his bed, still warm."

The man then knew that his brother had been trying to tell him that he was dying. He covered his brother's face, and braver than I would be, he went back upstairs for the night.

VOICES ON THE LABRADOR

Red Bay and Emily Harbour

Uncle Ambrose Powell, like many men along the Labrador Straits, was a fisherman in the warm weather, and in the colder months he worked his traplines. He had no family of his own, and his mother had passed away some time before. One spring, Uncle Ambrose went out to set his traps, and while on the trapline a strange, disembodied voice saved his life.

I heard the story of Uncle Ambrose from Alice Moores of Red Bay, who is a fine storyteller. Uncle Ambrose Powell was one of her ancestors, a Red Bay gentleman who died in the mid-1900s.

Once he arrived at his cabin on the trapline, Uncle Ambrose settled himself away and got his supper started. Outside, wind and wolves howled in the cold Labrador night.

"The tilt wasn't very tight," describes Moores, "so you had the wind whistling through the tilt, through the boards."

Suddenly, the man heard a voice.

"Like anyone would, he questioned what he was hearing, and he blamed it on the wind," Moores says, "but it seemed as if this particular voice was telling him 'Go home tomorrow, Ambrose.'"

The voice had a familiar ring to it, but he shrugged it off and went about his business.

"He got his supper ready, and he cleaned up from supper," continues Moores. "Then he settled back in the heat of the cabin. He had a nice fire going, and he smoked his pipe. He filled his pipe full of tobacco, and he set back to relax a bit after a long day's walk."

Uncle Ambrose was not settled long before he heard the voice again, a little bit closer.

"Go home tomorrow, Ambrose," said the voice.

"He thought about it," says Moores, "and the voice seemed to be a little bit familiar, but he still wasn't sure that it was anything to it, and he was still a little bit hesitant. So he said, 'If I hear this voice one more time, and I can recognize who it is that's talking to me, then maybe I'll listen.'"

The man did not hear anything else for a while. He got squared away into his bunk and settled down for the night. Everything was quiet except for the wind, which still howled mournfully outside.

Then he heard the voice again, this time quite loud and very close to his ear.

"Go home tomorrow, Ambrose."

"Yes, Mother," said Ambrose. "Tomorrow I'll go home."

"The next morning, Ambrose packed up all his things and set off to go home," says Moores. "He arrived home just shortly before spring broke, and he never returned to the country again.

"As far as I know, that is a true story. He did come home, and shortly after he got home, spring broke. If he hadn't come home, he would not have gotten home, because there are some very large rivers and brooks that you have to cross, and if they had broken up, there was just no way. He would have been stuck outside and perished then, for sure.

"That's the story of Ambrose."

Uncle Ambrose was not the only one to hear voices from beyond while exploring the wilds of Labrador. In 1949, a fifteen-year-old girl named Louise left Conception Bay to go up working on the Labrador for the first time. She set off with her father and three other men. Her father had a fishing room in a little place call Tar Barrel in Emily Harbour, five miles below Smokey on the way up to Nain. There, the girl worked cooking, working in the stage, splitting fish, and heading fish. As she put it, "whatever a man could do, I'd do it."

At the time that Louise and her father's crew were working on the Labrador, the fish was sold to J.W. Hiscock's in Brigus. A quintal (112 pounds) of dried fish would fetch between $4.50 to $5, if they were lucky. Much earlier, in the late 1800s, fish from Emily Harbour was sold to J. Munn and Company, with the agent at that time being George Apsey. James Ryan of Bonavista also had an economic interest in Emily Harbour, as his 1902 will and testament show that he and Daniel A. Ryan were equal partners in a mercantile premises at Emily Harbour.

Emily Harbour was a regular stop for the mail steamer which ran between the first week of July and ended about the first week of November. Emily Harbour was also noteworthy as being the final resting spot of the schooner *Shamrock* of the Rorke firm, which burnt in the harbour while loading fish.

There were thirty crews in the Emily Harbour area in the late 1940s and early '50s, but Louise spent most of her first days alone. Every morning, she would get up at four o'clock, make bread, scrub clothes with the washboard, and do other chores while the men went out jigging. They would return around one or two o'clock.

There were no roads between the different fishing rooms, only rabbit paths, which added to the sense of isolation. The girl's brother and one of the other fellows used this fact, combined with the girl's newness to the Labrador, to tease her and make her even more nervous than she had been to start.

"Now Louise, if you see a bear come ashore, go into the porch and throw the whole hundred pounds of beef out," they told her. That way she could run away and let the bear eat the beef, instead of her, presumably. As a result, she was scared to death. She was so frightened to be alone that she would get up out of her bed and crawl into her father's after everyone had left.

Every morning when the men went off fishing, she would get up and take out her father's twelve-gauge shotgun. She did not know how much powder went into it, so she poured in a generous helping, a bit of wadding, and a bunch of shot. With the loaded gun beside her, she felt much safer. Then each day before the men came back, she would go down on the stagehead, pull the trigger, and let it roar out over the water.

As the cook for the room, one of Louise's jobs was to make bread every day. To do this, she used one hundred pounds of flour a week. Around seven thirty in the morning, after she had made the bread for the day, she would go down to the stage to jig for fish.

One day as she went down on the stage, after she had

been there for about a week, she heard a voice say, clear as day, "When are you going home?"

The girl didn't think there was anyone in that area and looked around to see if someone had come up behind her. There was no one to be seen. The next day, she went back out on the stagehead. Once more, the unseen person called out asking, "When are you going home?"

The girl thought to herself, *I have to go and find out about this.*

Off she went, exploring. It was not long before she walked down into one of the nicest-looking places she had ever laid eyes on. It was a little gulch, with a beautiful sand beach and hills on both sides. Not more than fifty feet back from the beach were three grave markers. Try as she might, Louise could not read what was on the headstones, as they were far too weathered. She gently straightened the old headstones and headed back to the house.

Later her father told her that in the 1800s, a family had died in Emily Harbour of smallpox and that the family was buried on the Labrador. The little gulch that she had discovered was named Graveyard Cove. Up to this point, the girl had been scared, but she was not scared after she learned the story. She returned to Graveyard Cove and placed wildflowers on the three graves every day. The ghostly voices stopped, and the girl returned with flowers until the end of the summer when she sailed back home to Conception Bay.

In the 1950s, Louise returned to Emily Harbour with a husband and children of her own. She went down to the stage one morning and heard a baby crying. She had two children by this point, but the crying was not coming from either of her own. The sound was coming from a distance away, up on the back of the hill. So once more off she set in exploration and found that there was no one there.

For two or three days in a row, she heard the baby crying. Finally, she asked some of the older people about the unseen baby and its phantom cries. They told her that many years before, a woman in the community had buried a baby up on the back of the hill. Louise looked for the grave but was never able to find it. Local legend maintained that she was not the only one to hear the unearthly cries and that they were a common sound in the air of Emily Harbour.

Today, the entire community of Emily Harbour is a ghost of its former self. What was a bustling collection of fishing rooms is now a quiet place, its days of business and community life long faded. Its stories, however, echo to this day.

POOR JOE BENOIT

Garia Bay

While researching stories about ghosts and tokens, I discovered a tale from a community about which I knew nothing. Not a well-known name today, Garia was a small town located in Garia Bay on the south coast of Newfoundland, halfway between the communities of Harbour le Cou and La Poile.

The origin of the town's name was probably from the French word for "station." Explorer James Cook recorded one fishing stage in the area in 1765, but the first record of permanent inhabitants was the 1836 census, which indicated twelve inhabitants living in the town. The population peaked at just under 200 people in the 1860s, but in 1873, roughly three-quarters of the population left for work on Anticosti Island. McAlpine's 1894–97 Directory for the Burgeo and La Poile District shows only two inhabitants for Garia Bay, Joseph Collins and George Collins, both fishermen. Sometime after 1911, the place was abandoned.

In 1886, at the time when the community was in its decline, it was home to a telegraph repeating station for the North Line running to Bay St. George. The line had been established only a few years previously and would last for only a few more years. Christmastime of that year, a series of strange events unfolded in the dwindling town.

We know the story of what transpired in Garia Bay because of the writings of one man, Michael Francis Howley, a Roman Catholic priest, archbishop, and author. For many years, Howley lived and worked out of St. George's on the west coast, where he was a public figure in the social, economic, spiritual, and political life of the area. He was a contributor to many publications, and one of his stories about Garia was published in 1915, the year following his death, in a journal called *Christmas Bells*. The seasonal magazine was published by Gray and Goodland and contained assorted articles, stories, bits of poetry, and photographs.

"The distance from Garia Station to Sandy Point was about fifty miles," wrote Howley in the publication, "and is certainly one of the most dreary and dangerous sections in Newfoundland, passing, as it does, right through the heart of the country over the lofty 'Long Range.'"

In 1886, the Garia telegraph station's company consisted of the operator with his wife and children, the line repairman Paul Benoit and his wife, Paul's younger brother Joe, "a fine strapping young fellow of twenty one years of age, newly broken in to the repairing business," and a few Mi'kmaq trappers in from their lines.

With the crew gathered there, word came in that there was a break in the line north of the station. The repairman, Paul Benoit, did not relish leaving the station and his wife at Christmastime. His brother Joe said that he would go, and off he set, borrowing both Paul's gun and his dog.

Here, we shall let Archbishop Howley take up the tale.

"On the following night, about two o'clock, when all at

the station were locked in slumber, Paul and his wife were awakened by hearing the well-known short, quick step of Joe on the crisp ground without. Then they heard him approach the door and turn the knob. They also heard the dog scraping at the door and whining. Paul was out of bed in a minute."

"Get up," he said to his wife, "and make down a fire, here's Joe—I'd know his step among a thousand."

"Yes," she said, "I heard him. I'll have the kettle boiled in no time; I suppose the poor fellow is starved."

While she was making the fire and getting some supper ready, Paul went out. He opened the door but found no one there. He went around the house, but there was no sign of either dog nor man. He called out loud and went along the path some distance, shouting, but found nothing. He returned to the house breathless and pale.

"It's all over with poor Joe," he told his wife.

'"What is it? Where is he? Why don't you bring him in?" she asked.

"Oh, he's far enough away from here," said Paul. "But he's dead as sure as I am alive, and that was his death token we heard."

They did not sleep again that night, and at daylight, Paul started off along the line with a pounding heart. Fourteen miles out, he discovered signs of Joe's presence. Joe had made a splice in the telegraph line and had stopped into a nearby tilt, a small rough cabin. But there was no sign of Joe, so Paul kept going.

Toward evening he found himself in a thick grove of woods. When night fell it was dark, without moon or stars. But strangely, the pathway before him was lit by some unseen source. First Paul found his gun, placed across the path in such a manner that it would be impossible for one to pass by without stumbling over it. Then he found Joe's snowshoes, one on top of the other across the path.

Paul came to a low gulch or valley about fifty yards across, where the strange light seemed brighter than ever. There lay his brother, lying peacefully across the path, with the dog standing over him and whining piteously. Howley describes the sad scene thusly,

"He had kneeled down to pray; the mark of his knees was in the soft ground. His left hand was stretched out and his cap near it, showing that he had taken it off to pray. His right hand was by his side and held his Rosary beads. . . . He did not die of hunger; he had plenty of 'grub' with him. There was some porridge left in his can, and he had bread enough."

Paul tore off a piece of his shirt to cover Joe's face. He then took his brother on his shoulders and carried him back to the tilt, laid him out, and waited alongside the corpse till daybreak.

In the morning, Paul started for Garia.

"It was then the faithful dog began to show the most pitiful signs of sorrow and attachment," writes Howley. "He would run ten or fifteen yards from the tilt, then stand on hind legs, paw the air, moan and whine in the most heart-rending manner and run back to the tilt, looking backwards towards his master as if it were beseeching him not to abandon the poor dead man. It was with the greatest difficulty Paul got him away from the tilt."

On arriving at Garia, Paul telegraphed his family in Bay St. George. A party of men set out carrying boards and nails to make a coffin. By the time Paul returned to the tilt, he found about fourteen men there. They made a rough coffin, and slinging it on a couple of rails, set out on their long funereal procession back to Bay St. George.

"And here again, it is the belief of all present, from many of whom the present writer has frequently heard it, that the supernatural element entered in," states Howley. "For they travelled without the slightest difficulty the whole length of that long thirty miles, bearing their heavy burthen through swamps, over brooks, across snow-banks, without difficulty or accident of any kind, and without in snow or bog in a manner which under ordinary circumstances would be altogether impossible."

The cause of death for poor Joe Benoit was never determined, and his last days remain shrouded in mystery. He was, in the final words of the archbishop, "a good and innocent young man. He now sleeps in peace in the blessed ground of the little graveyard at St. George's awaiting the trumpet-call, and the reward of 'the good and faithful servant.'"

THE PREMONITION OF THE SOUTHERN CROSS

TRINITY AND BIRCHY COVE, TRINITY BAY

Every part of Newfoundland and Labrador has its own tradition of strange nautical tales, and Trinity Bay is no exception. A number of local spirits were recorded for posterity in 1925 by William White (1860–1949). A native of Trinity, Trinity Bay, William White devoted much time in his later years to the collection and recording of local and church history, and he documented a number of ghost stories, including a ghost ship seen by a local man nicknamed "Crusty Harry."

Stories of wrecks and ghost ships continue to be told in Trinity Bay. Garland Bailey of the Trinity Historical Society told me of a skeleton-like ghost ship that was said to appear sailing up Trinity Bay. What made the story novel to me was that the ship was said to only have its wooden ribs, missing its planking.

One of the more intriguing shipwreck stories I have heard from Trinity Bay was one I learned from Shirley Ryan of Birchy Cove. Her tale is a mysterious one, involving one of Newfoundland's famous lost ships, the *Southern Cross*, and the different fates of two friends, Edmund Ryan and Leonard Skiffington.

"Now, Edmund Ryan was my girlfriend's grandfather who lived just down across the garden, so to us he was Uncle Ned," she explains. "Uncle Ned always told the story about how he and Leonard left Birchy Cove, where he lived, to go across to Catalina. They were really lucky; they had gotten a berth on the *Southern Cross.*

"They left Birchy Cove and they made their way to Catalina," she describes. "I think they went over on a dogsled, maybe, because there were no cars to bring them at that time, and the road across the country was little better than a path."

The two men arrived in Catalina and were about to sign on.

"They had their berth already promised," says Ryan. "They went into what he used to call a tavern. I've never known a tavern to be there, but maybe in them days there were. They went into this tavern to get a drink. Water was all they could afford. They had no money. So they asked the woman there for a glass of water each, and she gave them the water."

When Uncle Ned turned, his arm knocked the glass onto the floor, breaking the woman's glass.

"You have to pay for that glass," she said to him.

He said, "Madam, I can't pay, I have no money."

"Where are you going?" the woman asked.

"We are going on the *Southern Cross.* We have a berth on the *Southern Cross.*"

"If you're wise, you won't go on that journey," the woman said, "because you won't return."

"Now, he was a man of great superstitions, and he took

what she said to heart, and he came home," describes Ryan. "But his friend Leonard wouldn't listen to him, and he went on that ship."

The *Southern Cross* was built in Norway in 1886 and was originally named the *Pollux*. She was sold to the Newfoundland firm of Baine Johnston and renamed the SS *Southern Cross* around 1901, and she took part in the seal hunt every year from 1901 to 1914. While returning from the seal hunt in the final days of March 1914, the *Southern Cross* fell out of normal communication. She was last heard off Cape Pine, and then, nothing.

Expedition ship SS Southern Cross, *1898.*
Photo courtesy State Library of Tasmania.

The *Southern Cross* vanished at sea, along with the 174 sailors and sealers on board her, part of the great sealing disasters of 1914. Eventually, a marine court of inquiry determined that the ship sank in a blizzard on March 31, but the details remain, for the most part, unexplained. No crewmen nor record of the ill-fated voyage survived. Among the list of the dead was one Leonard Skiffington, originally of Newman's Cove, Bonavista Bay.

"Uncle Ned told us that story over and over and over," says Ryan. "It's a true story. He told it over and over, about how he took what she said as serious and accused her of being a witch. Well, lots of people were accused of being witches them days! But he said the woman that owned that tavern was a witch, and when she said that, that was enough for him. He didn't go.

"But Leonard did go, and, well, Leonard never returned," Ryan states. "Nobody ever returned, eh? That's my little story."

The Newfoundland sealing disaster is such an important part of our literary and oral traditions in the province that it is unsurprising that a number of supernatural tales have attached themselves to the disaster. I suspect the story here is just one of many told by the descendants of the men who were lost on the ice or in the wreck of the *Southern Cross.*

A SMELL OF DEATH

Spaniard's Bay and Carbonear

Often, the stories I hear about the supernatural or the paranormal are either visual or auditory. People see ghostly figures or hear strange noises in the night. Sometimes people might have some kind of tactile experience: a ghost might touch someone on the shoulder, or a haunted house might develop strange cold spots.

Smells are another way people experience the unknown. I have heard eerie stories about someone catching a whiff of their long-departed grandfather's pipe tobacco or their auntie's favourite perfume. People have told me stories of smelling smoke where there was no fire and smelling a dead brother's cologne.

In 2014, folklorist Lisa Wilson and I worked with students at Ascension Collegiate in Bay Roberts, helping them research local folk beliefs. One student from Upper Island Cove, Ryan Adams, wrote about a strange odour associated with a night terror.

"I woke up and I couldn't move and there was a weird smell, like old clothes, and it felt like someone was in the room with me," Adams wrote. "I believe it was just a dream."

A few years later, I was back in that part of the province, giving a talk on folk belief and superstitions for the Heritage Society in Spaniard's Bay at the Wesley Gosse Memorial Building (the old United Church). There was a lively discussion from the crowd, with many stories told about various bits and pieces of local folklore. Afterwards, one woman approached me and asked if I had ever come across a story about someone who could smell death approaching.

She went on to explain that a woman she knew had been born with the ability to smell death. From time to time the woman would smell a very particular scent, and each time the odour appeared, a death would follow.

One day, she told her husband she had smelled that scent again, but stronger than she had smelled it before, almost enough to turn her stomach. A short time afterwards, the woman herself died, perhaps unaware that the death which she had smelled approaching had been her own.

It was a tiny story, but it immediately caught my imagination. A lot of the stories I hear follow predictable patterns or incorporate common motifs, but the idea of a smell being a token or premonition of death is not one I had previously come across.

I went looking for others with this strange ability. Sure enough, on the online nursing forum allnurses.com, one registered nurse wrote the following:

"I first noticed it when I was in nursing school, and we were orienting on the floor. We would go in a room with a patient, and I would smell this sickly sweet odour, and around a week later, the patient would be dead. It continues to this day. I have smelled Lord knows how many smells, but this one almost defies description."

Other nurses have reported the same thing, that they can detect a specific odour around patients about to die. Other people have reported the scent of roses as a sign that someone near to them will soon pass on.

A short drive north of Spaniard's Bay, about twenty kilometres or so, is the town of Carbonear. Here, too, are those who say they can pick out the scent of oncoming death.

"I can smell it in the air of their room," a Carbonear woman told me. "It lingers in the air."

The woman who told me this had been a care worker at a private nursing home in Carbonear. Her uncanny ability to sense when someone was about to die was something she discovered early on.

"I noticed it was something I could tell at a young age. I used to ask my mom if she could smell it in the room, thinking it was something normal. It smells somewhat funeral-home-like: of carnations, roses, and incense. Usually, they have a grey cast around them. I used to tell my mom and my nan that, and they used to say that I should work with elderly people, or in a profession where I helped people. I worked for a little while with elderly people. I remember one lady, I went in to get her up for breakfast and I went in her room and that's all I could smell. I knew; I told my mom when I went home. She died two days later."

Travis George Parsons lives in Grand Bank, but his mother's side of the family were Chants from La Poile on the south coast.

"We recently found out a couple of years ago that there is a lot of Mi'kmaq blood in the family up there," he told me. "My grandmother, her daughters (my mother and aunts), and my sister have all experienced this experience of 'smelling' death."

For the ladies of the Chant family, it is best explained as a scent, or even a passing impression of a smell, which they pick up on before someone passes away.

"It's clear to them what they are 'smelling' as they smell it, even if they didn't experience it before," explains Parsons. "On several occasions, all of these family members have been in the presence of someone and had this happen. A short time after, something has happened to this person, or a friend or family member of this person.

"I distinctly remember as a child that my sister's friend was in my grandmother's porch talking to her as she was leaving. When she left, my sister said she smelled death as her friend was talking in the porch. I was only young then, and it startled me. I asked a lot of questions about it as my entire life was consumed by these superstitions and omens. That night, that person's uncle died suddenly. I'll never forget it."

"Animals are said to be able to do this as well," one of my interviewees told me, a statement which I heard from several people when asking about the ability. Dogs, cats, and even horses have been said to have the ability to sniff out certain cancers and to be able to identify the dying and nearly dead.

The most famous of these animal prognosticators of death was a cat by the name of Oscar, who lived in a nursing home in Rhode Island, USA. The cat was said to be notoriously anti-social but would cuddle up to residents in their final dying days. Dr. David Dosa wrote about Oscar's abilities in the *New England Journal of Medicine* in 2007 and later told the UK publication the *Mirror Online*, "He only comes to the 'end of life' patients who are near death. I think he is attracted in some capacity to them. I think he probably is responding to a pheromone or a scent."

Dosa wrote in his 2007 report: "His mere presence at the bedside is viewed by physicians and nursing home staff as an almost absolute indicator of impending death, allowing staff members to adequately notify families." As of January 2010, Oscar was said to have predicted approximately fifty patients' deaths.

But you do not have to go all the way to Rhode Island to meet such a talented cat. A St. John's cat named Purrl had a similar capability. As my friend Sara told me,

"When Mom was in her last few days our old cat Purrl, who was probably about twenty-two at the time, came into her room and curled up at the foot of her bed. The cat didn't move for forty-eight hours, and then a few moments after Mom passed, the cat got up, jumped off the bed, and walked to the other end of the house."

So, is smelling the scent of impending death a supernatural power, or a fine-tuned biological response to changes in pheromones or body chemistry? Only Oscar and Purrl know for sure.

SAYING FAREWELL

Islington

If you were given the option to be able to sense when someone in your community was going to die, is that a gift you would want to accept? And how would you feel if you had no choice in the matter at all?

In the fall of 2016, Pauline Chislett Masters mentioned to me in passing that she had a supernatural story to tell me. I am not one to pass up hearing a new story, so we arranged to meet at her office. There, she told me a story about a ghostly visitor and about an uncanny ability to sense an oncoming death.

Masters grew up in the community of Islington, Trinity Bay. While her family never told ghost stories or spooky tales to frighten the children, they would oftentimes talk of tokens, supernatural signs of an impending death.

"Mom mentioned a few times about seeing a token or hearing a token," says Masters. "If something fell down in the back room, or something fell off a shelf, they'd say, 'Oh, that could be a token; I wonder who is going to die this time?'"

As a girl, she would go weekly to visit her grandmother.

"I can't remember a lot about her, but I know we used to visit every Sunday," she remembers. "She was originally from Cavendish, but when she got well into her seventies, she went to live with Aunt Esther, at Eastern Corner in Whiteway.

"Mom would gather up the troops, and she'd take us up to see Grandmother. I always sat on her lap. She always had her arms open for me when I walked through the door. I was probably three or four. She'd put me on her lap, and that's where I'd spend my day, on Grandmother's lap, and she'd be rocking in the rocking chair. That was the only thing I remember doing with my grandmother, because she died when I was eleven or something."

The day after her grandmother died, the girl went to bed, where she slept till she woke in the middle of the night.

"I woke up and my room was all lit up," Masters says. "I haven't told this; even my family don't know! I was on my side facing the wall. I turned, and there was my grandmother. She was sitting on the bed, and everything was all lit up. Now, at the time, Mom didn't believe in letting children go to funerals. I wanted to go to the funeral, but she wouldn't let me go. I was upset over it, certainly, but that was all you could do."

The ghostly grandmother looked at the girl and smiled.

"She put her hand on my leg as if to say, 'Everything is okay.' I just kept watching her," says Masters. "I wasn't scared—you would think I would be—and she just stared at me with a big smile on her face and just faded away. That was very weird. I never said anything, because I know people would say, 'Yeah, right!'

"It was like she had come to say goodbye because I hadn't been to her funeral. The last time I had seen her, she had Alzheimer's, so she didn't know who I was."

Since that eventful day, Masters seems to have inherited the ability to sense when someone near is going to die.

"It's creepy," she confesses. "I don't know who it is, but I know when someone is going to die. It is going to be quick, and most times it is tragic. It could be someone close or someone well-known. It is either someone tapping me on the shoulder or the feeling as if someone is following me around. It is the same sensation, all the time. It is like someone is there, trying to tell me something. It actually feels like someone is right tight behind me. When the person dies, it goes away. I've never told anyone that, except a couple of my friends, but that's it."

While visiting one of those friends, she was standing in the doorway getting ready to leave.

"We were just chatting," she describes. "I said, 'I'll talk to you tomorrow,' and it felt like somebody tapped me on my shoulder. I turned around, I turned the other way, and I looked. I turned back and looked at my friend. 'Oh no,' she said. 'Yep,' I said, 'someone is going to die.' 'My God,' she said, 'I wish you'd stop doing that!' Two or three days later, there was a guy from Heart's Delight who was killed by a transport truck."

The premonitions have happened a few times over the years, with the last occurrence in September of 2016.

"I was up berry picking behind the house in the fall," she describes. "For the whole day it was like someone was following me, and I knew what was coming. Every time I go berry picking, my two cats come with me, and they wouldn't come with me. They stayed home, and I thought maybe the coyotes were around again. I had to come down; I was creeped right out. It was like somebody was behind me.

"When I got home, that night, my girlfriend called me and said this woman from Islington had passed away. They had found her dead in her own bed.

"It's very weird; I don't like it," she told me, when I asked what it felt like.

"Can you make it go away?"

ONE FOR SORROW

Marystown, Spaniard's Bay, Bay Roberts, South River, Cape la Hune, and Doctor's Harbour

What do you do when you see a single crow?

"Oh, I cross that thing out right away!" laughs Christa Marshall. "It was something my friends and I did in high school, in Marystown. 'One for sorrow, two for joy . . .' I believe one of my friends had learned it from her mother."

Marshall is not alone in this custom. In many communities in Newfoundland, people have a tradition of "crossing out" a single crow, raising a finger to make the sign of a cross or an X in the air when one is spotted. One Mi'kmaq man told me he always crosses out a single crow and pushes it to the side.

"Always!" he added.

Some blink, so they "see" two birds instead of one. One woman told me she makes an X three times; another said she crosses it out nine times, and then, if she sees another, she licks her finger and makes a cross on something blue, a process which seems incredibly time-consuming to me.

Others cry out "Hey Mr. Crow, where's your friend?" while one man told me that every crow is born with a drop of the Devil's blood, hence the need to make the sign of the cross in the first place.

"I remember my aunt telling me that she crosses them out as well," adds Marshall. "But to be subtle, she sometimes just winks one eye and then the other so that it's 'less noticeable!'"

The magpie. Illustration by Thomas Bewick, 1809.

All these winking, crossing, pushing, and licking traditions seems to have English origins surrounding traditional folk beliefs about magpies. According to a BBC website,

> . . . one magpie on its own is a sign of bad luck. There is no known reason for this superstition, but it is very common. There are various things you can do if you meet a single magpie in order to ward off the bad luck. These

include taking your hat off and making the sign of the cross, spitting three times over your shoulder, and saluting the magpie with "Hello Mr. Magpie, How's your lady wife today?"

When settlers came to Newfoundland, there were no magpies, but there were plenty of crows, so the folklore shifted from magpies to the local bird.

This adaptation can be seen in another bit of traditional lore, namely crow counting rhymes. Rhymes for counting magpies can be found in written form all the way back to the 1600s. Once the rhyme crossed the Atlantic, crows were substituted. The late Mr. Wesley Gosse, who was born in 1935 in Spaniard's Bay, was a great source for old place names, rhymes, and folklore of the Spaniard's Bay area. One of the rhymes he had collected caught my interest in particular. It was about counting crows as a means of foretelling the future, and as I remember his words, it went like this:

One for fair,
Two for wet.
Three for sickness,
Four for death.
Five for a funeral.

I had heard other versions of the counting-out rhyme, but I had never heard this particular version from Spaniard's Bay. When I asked around, other people had heard many other versions, the most popular being:

One for sorrow,
Two for joy,
Three for a girl,
Four for a boy,
Five for silver,
Six for gold,
Seven for a secret (or story) never to be told.

One contact from Bay Roberts wrote me to say that "everyone in Newfoundland knows" that one crow equals sorrow; two crows, joy; and that three foretell a wedding. "Everyone" is perhaps a bit of an exaggeration, and what seems more accurate is that the rhyme is found in various (and sometimes wildly different) versions in different communities and different areas. Paula Roberts of Clarenville learned a version from a cousin in South River as a child. Her rhyme started:

One for sorrow,
Two for joy,
Three for a kiss,
Four for a boy.

In their book *The Lore and Language of Schoolchildren*, Iona and Peter Opie include the English counting rhyme, "one crow for sorrow, two for joy, three for a letter, four for a boy" and note that, in Wales, two black crows equal good luck. The longest version of the counting-crows rhyme I know came to me through Memorial University folklore student Rebekah Nolan, who had a fantastic version. She learned it in San Luis Obispo, California, circa 2003:

One for sadness
Two for mirth
Three for marriage
Four for birth
Five for laughing
Six for crying
Seven for sickness
Eight for dying
Nine for silver
Ten for gold
Eleven for a secret that will never be told
Twelve for darkness
Thirteen for light
Fifteen for morning
Sixteen for night

In 1895, a man by the name of George Patterson from New Glasgow, Nova Scotia, wrote an article called "Notes on the Folk-Lore of Newfoundland" for the *Journal of American Folklore.* Patterson was primarily interested in superstitions and folk beliefs and collected many of his stories from one Judge Bennett of Harbour Grace. At that time and in that place, older magpie customs had shifted to another locally available bird, the pigeon.

"Meeting a tame pigeon is unlucky," wrote Patterson. "If a single pigeon crosses a lady's pathway, she may anticipate sorrow as near, but two together is a sign of coming joy, three promise a wedding, and four a birth."

Another intriguing pigeon belief was reported in the same journal in 1896:

"At Cape la Hune I heard more superstitions than I could tell in an hour. I was assured of . . . people unable to die lying on pigeons' feathers, and the feathers removed, they die easily."

While counting pigeons or crows might be one way of foretelling the future in many Newfoundland settlements, in the early part of the twentieth century, a single loon was said to be a sign of trouble to come in the now-abandoned community of Doctor's Harbour.

Doctor's Harbour was located in Fortune Bay between Rencontre East and Belleoram. A local legend concerned a loon with a very peculiar, shrill call. Sometimes in the spring or summer of the year, men out in their boats would see the loon come up out of the water, making its unique sound. The loon would never be seen more than three times any given day.

If the loon was sighted, it was a sure sign that rain and strong winds from the south would follow within one day. Belief in the ability of the loon to predict a storm was so strong that, if one boat came ashore saying they had seen the bird, everyone else out on the water would hurry to haul up his boat as well.

One version of the legend says that the loon was no ordinary bird at all but was rather the ghost of a French fisherman. The unfortunate man had been stabbed with what is known variously in Newfoundland as a fish-fork, pew, or sprong: a long stick with one or two tines used in transferring codfish from boat to fishing stage.

After his murder, the Frenchman's body had been dumped overboard. For whatever reason, his ghost returned to haunt the bay in the shape of a loon. Some said that, after a dive, the loon took on the shape of a fish-fork as it left the water.

While death-proof pigeon-feather beds and weather-predicting loons may be part of the folklore of the past, the practice of crossing out crows seems to be here to stay.

CHAPTER TWO
Shades of Yesteryear

My sister-in-law Grace was living in on the hill. It was a rainy night, and I thought "I better go in and see how Grace is getting on." So I took the lantern and went on in; there were no flashlights in those days. I went in and stayed till eleven o'clock, and when I came out it was raining harder than ever.

She came out on the bridge with me and watched me walk back down. I got down over the hill, and called back at her, "You go in the house now, because I'm not afraid." I was quite brave, you know!

She went in the house, and I walked perhaps twenty or thirty yards till I came to a little bridge across the brook.

All of a sudden, such a funny feeling came over me, and it seemed as if my hair stood on end. I could scarcely move my legs along. At last I got down to turn up the hill toward home, and once I got opposite one of the flakes there, someone kicked my heel.

Perhaps you have been walking in a crowd and have felt somebody kick your heel. I glanced back over my shoulder, and I didn't see anything. When I got to the top of the hill and saw my sister-in-law's light in the house, the sensation went, and I was perfectly natural again.

What do you make of that? There was something there that kicked my heel. It gave me a fright. I never went there by myself in the night for four years after that!

— Adapted from a story told by Mrs. Beatrice Toope of Ireland's Eye to broadcaster Hiram Silk, 1969

The Radiant Boy. Illustration by Horace Castelli, circa 1880.

FERRIES AND PHANTOM FERRYMEN

Bell Island, St. John's, and Trinity, Trinity Bay

I could never write about Newfoundland and Labrador folklore without including a few ghost ship stories. There is no shortage of stories of ghost ships from the province, and one typical example is that of a large white steamer, described by author Horace Beck.

"She is usually seen in the offing making for a harbour too small to hold her," writes Beck. "Nevertheless, on she comes under a full head of steam, enters the harbour, runs up on the shore, and keeps going 'cross lots.'"

Older readers with knowledge of Bell Island and surroundings may have memories of retired ferries like the *Kipawa* and the *John Guy*, but it was the ferry the SS *Mary* that had a run-in with another ghostly steamer.

"Another famous name made its appearance in local shipping circles in the summer of 1907," writes Addison Bown. "SS *Mary* was purchased in Quebec by the Bell Island Steamship Company and used at first as a freighter between St. John's and the Island. When she arrived off the beach in August that year with her first cargo, she was too big to berth at the public wharf and the freight had to be discharged in boats and lighters. The *Mary* replaced the *Progress* on the Tickle in September when the latter went to St. John's for refit."

The SS *Mary* was licensed to carry sixty passengers, and initial response to the ship seems to have been positive, though she soon ran into a few problems.

The "Harbor Grace Notes" section of the *Evening Telegram* for August 27 of that year relates: "The Bell Island steamer *Mary* arrived from the Island on Saturday last with a number of passengers, men who came home to spend Sunday with their friends. The *Mary* is a most suitable boat for the service, and the workmen are delighted with the opportunity of spending Sunday at home. . . . On Sunday evening she returned to take the men back to the island, and while being berthed she struck the public wharf, damaging it somewhat."

Captain of a ship, unidentified. Photo 12.09.001, courtesy Sir Robert Bond Collection (Coll-237), Archives and Special Collections, Memorial University.

By November, the steamer had run into trouble again. As the *Evening Telegram* reported on November 9, "Yesterday she grounded near the wharf that is built out from the beach at the island and had one of her propeller blades broken. Capt. Dawe asked us to say that if the wharf was ten feet longer it would not have happened, and he strongly recommends this addition."

The damage could not have been extensive, as the *Mary* was back in service by December, making runs to Harbour Grace, Carbonear, Bell Island, and into St. John's.

It was on one of these runs into St. John's that the SS *Mary* had an encounter with what some of the crew believed to be a ghost ship. A few days after Christmas, the ship was almost run down by a ship which vanished in a strange fashion.

On December 28, 1907—in a short article entitled "What Was It?"—the *Evening Telegram* reported the event as follows:

> The crew of the steamer *Mary*, which arrived from Bell Island at midnight last night, told us today that before they entered the Narrows, a large steamer was seen by them in the strain off Black Head with red and blue lights hoist in her rigging. She came like a flash toward them, and the engineer of the *Mary* thought that they would be run down. She passed, so he states, at the rate of twenty-five miles an hour, and the most mysterious thing about her was that they lost sight of her after she got near Sugar Loaf; she disappeared from view. They are conjecturing today what ship it was and whether it was a phantom ship or not. The engineer said that he never witnessed the like of such a scene in all the years he has been going to sea.
>
> "We thank the crew for this Xmas Ghost Story," added the anonymous writer of the article.

While ferry passengers around St. John's might have seen a phantom steamer, the town of Trinity, Trinity Bay, has a ghostly ferryman. The story was originally collected by broadcaster Hiram Silk, as told to him by Beatrice Toope of Ireland's Eye. In the early part of the twentieth century, an outport girl named Grace moved from her community to work in the town of Trinity, Trinity Bay. While there, she lived with her aunt and uncle.

One evening in February, the aunt went up to a friend's house and stayed to tea. When she went up, she did not intend to stay, so she did not have a light with her.

Time passed, and when Grace came home from work, it was quite dark

"Go up and carry the light and fetch your aunt home," said her uncle.

It was a slippery night, with ice snow on the ground, but off she set with flashlight in hand. Around seven o'clock, she came to the house with a white picket fence where her aunt had stayed for tea. As soon as she came in through the gate in the fence, a strange thing happened.

Grace heard a little noise, and she looked toward the woodhouse. She turned her flashlight toward the woodhouse to see if there was anybody there, but she saw no one. Then she turned the light onto the fence.

There, on the other side of the fence, she saw something like a man's face and figure, with the body resting its arms on the face. She could not see the lower part of its body, but she saw a face with long, white whiskers. The figure wore an old-fashioned hat with a shiny bill, like the style of hat a captain might wear.

Grace managed to get into the house, and when she

came in, the aunt saw immediately that there was something wrong.

"What's wrong with you, maid?" the aunt asked. "Who was chasing you? What did you see?"

"I didn't see anybody living," said the girl, after a pause.

"I suppose you didn't see anybody dead, then," said the aunt, but the girl made no response.

The two women said their farewells and left. They came down the path, and as they did, Grace flashed her light up and down the fence.

"Put your light down on the ground," said the aunt, uncomprehending. "That's where I'm going to tread!"

"When I get up over this hill, I'm going to tell you something," said Grace.

True to her word, when they got up over the hill, and away from the property, Grace described what she had seen, down to the whiskers and the billed cap.

"But it was nothing living, with such a strange face," said Grace.

The next day the aunt decided to find out if someone had died in that house or if there was a similar story. She went over to a neighbour and asked who had died in the house.

"Oh yes," said the neighbour. "Old Bobby died there."

The aunt asked what he had looked like.

"Well, he had long, white whiskers, and any time you saw him, he had a cap on," said the neighbour. "He used to run the ferry that went up the Southwest Arm, and when he was an old man he went to live with his daughter. Every evening, just about seven or seven thirty, he'd go outdoors and lean on the fence and look up the arm, just to check on the ferry."

MRS. KING'S HOUSE

Boyd's Cove

How would you feel if a group of strangers suddenly moved into your house? If you are like Mrs. King, you probably would not approve.

The Waterman family was building a winter tilt, and they had no place to live while the work was under way. A nearby resident, Mr. King, had moved out of his house after the death of his wife, and as it was vacant, he offered it to the Watermans temporarily.

"We went there one night and it was all right, best kind," says Aunt Jessie Waterman. "Then the next night we went to bed, and someone came and stood over me, a woman. But I didn't mind that. I just turned inside and went to sleep. I never spoke of it; it wasn't a dream."

On the third night, however, things went from bad to worse.

"Mrs. King was dead then. She didn't want us there. She didn't want anyone there," says Aunt Jessie. "There was always something telling me not to touch anything that belonged to her.

"And then the next night we went to bed and we had to

get up. There was a wonderful noise in the house that evening, heaving chairs and everything. That's what it seemed like, to us. So we had to leave that night, and get up and dress the youngsters and row across the cove in boat over to Mrs. Mugford's."

It was raining, with the wind up from the east. But they put the children in the boat and made their way to the safety of the Mugfords'. When they arrived in the middle of the storm, Mrs. Mugford said she had known they were not going to last long in the King household. She told the Watermans that she too had seen the spirit of old Mrs. King, who would come down and lean over the fence, and then vanish up in the air like a ball of fire.

"It didn't want us to stay in the house," says Aunt Jessie. "That was her way to get us out of the house. It didn't want anyone living there. Even her husband, he couldn't live in it."

THE GHOST OF MRS. PRIDE

PILLEY'S ISLAND

The community of Tilt Cove, Notre Dame Bay, was first settled around 1813 or earlier by George and Mary Winsor from the West Country England. Originally a fishing settlement, the town grew after the discovery of copper ore in the area in 1857 led to the development of a mine in 1864. The mine, opened by Smith McKay and C. F. Bennett, brought prosperity to the town, and by 1916, the population had grown to 1500.

In 1986, ninety-eight-year-old Jack Mansfield, originally of Tilt Cove, was interviewed for a local radio program. The son of a miner, Mansfield, at age sixteen, moved with his family to Pilley's Island, another mining community. The Tilt Cove mine, however, closed for good in 1908. Young Mansfield worked in the local sawmills, preparing wood for use in schooner building, and then later working on the railway, laying rails. Later in life, he worked as a teamster in the lumber camps for the Anglo-Newfoundland Development Company.

In the radio interview, Mansfield shared stories and memories of life in the early twentieth century. One of those stories was about the ghost of a woman by the name of Mrs.

Pride, with whom he had an encounter in Pilley's Island.

"I came down over what they called The Route, down over Taylor's Hill," said Mansfield, who had been heading to a spot to get a drink of beer. Coming up the hill, he had passed a spot where a woman had been seen many times.

"Tilt Cove, N.D. Bay looking outward—noted for its valuable copper mine," photograph of an engraving, circa 1900. Image courtesy Archives and Special Collections, Memorial University.

"She was there, coming toward me when I was going up the grade," said Mansfield. "She was a dead person. . . . I could see her with her hair parted in the centre, that old-style part.

"I knew it from the rig she had on," he said, explaining how he knew her to be a ghost. "She had on what they'd call a nightdress, and long nightdress, right down, right down to her feet.

"It never frightened me one bit! Only, I turned around and went on home.

"When I looked over my shoulder, she was facing the road, looking up and down the road," Mansfield related.

"When I looked, she was looking at me going down the road. She turned around. I know she turned around. Anyway, I went down as far as I could, to see if she was going to go down the main road. She never went on the main road. She must have went back to the graveyard again, wherever the graveyard was."

At that point, she vanished.

According to the folklore of Pilley's Island, the figure of the woman in the nightdress was the spirit of a local lady, Mrs. Pride.

"Mrs. Pride died in her house, just like anyone else," said Mansfield, but for some reason she returned to haunt the community and was seen by "lots of young men."

"Some got frightened and ran away, frightened to death, fainted off, and all this," he said. "I never did!"

In the 1920s, Mansfield had a run-in with another ghost, that of an old French lumberman, while working in the woods on the west coast of Newfoundland. Mansfield saw the phantom logger coming along the trail at dawn, wearing lumbering clothes and a scarf about his neck, near the spot where he was said to be buried.

Mansfield claims he knew the figure was a ghost, but he was not frightened by that phantom either, though some of the other loggers were spooked by the story.

"I know a lot of the fellows wouldn't get out of the bunk to make their water, they were that much afraid," he said. "I thinks they'd seen something."

THE MORTUARY WREATH

Crouse

Originally known as Cap Rouge, the little community of Crouse on Newfoundland's Great Northern Peninsula housed an important French fishing station in the late nineteenth century. English and Irish settlement came later, and for years French fishing crews came from St. Malo to fish the waters off the coast of Newfoundland and Labrador.

The interactions between the French and the Newfoundlanders gave rise to many stories, including one particularly interesting ghost story. The story was recorded by Alicia Norris in the *Atlantic Guardian* magazine in 1946. Norris had learned the story from an old fisherman in Crouse, fluent in French, who had sailed with the foreign crews as a boy.

In 1879, the French fleet arrived in early May, with the barquentine *Sainte Marie* being the first to reach land. Each ship tried to reach Newfoundland first, as the captain of the first ship would become the Admiral of the Fleet for that fishing season. Le Capitaine Henri Lajeunesse was captain of the *Sainte Marie*, but his tenure as fishing admiral was short-lived: after only a day in Newfoundland, Lajeunesse died.

Sailing ships at anchor, 1857–59, South West Crouse. Photo courtesy Library and Archives Canada—Bibliothèque et Archives Canada PA-188223.

The admiral was buried in Crouse, and the French fished all season, returning to St. Malo at the end of the year. But the next year, when they returned, locals were surprised to see them approach the shore with a priest standing in the rowboat. The priest led a procession to the grave and began a funeral service for the admiral, who had died the summer previously. At the culmination of the ceremony, a curious box was brought forward and opened.

"With due formality, from its box and wrappings, was unfolded a huge, multicoloured, china mortuary wreath of indescribable beauty," writes Norris. "It was lovingly inscribed from the wife and children of the dead seaman. The priest laid it on the grave and blessed it. The congregation sang 'La Marseillaise' and dispersed."

"An object of such beauty had rarely been seen in Crouse," adds Norris. "People came from miles around to admire it with almost as much sense of possession as did the French sailors who stood pridefully by."

During the winter months, a local family was given the honour of moving the wreath from the grave to their house for safekeeping. Each summer, it was returned to the grave. This process continued unhindered for several years. But one summer morning, when the son of the family charged with the care of the wreath went to the graveyard, the wreath was missing.

According to local legend, the wreath was stolen by some of the men of the fishing schooner *Daisy May*. It was a theft that did not go down well with some of the crew; one older gentleman was said to have crossed himself, denounced the men as desecrators, and predicted that bad luck would follow.

True to the man's prediction, ill luck followed shortly. The fish vanished, replaced with nothing but fog. The schooner ran up on a shoal, then later was caught in terrible storms. One of the best sailors on the crew was tossed from the rigging by unseen hands and fell to the deck with a smashed leg and broken ribs. Another young man was partially blinded after a close call with a bolt of lightning.

Before long, the crew was certain that the enraged ghost of Le Capitaine Henri Lajeunesse stalked the ship from stem to stern. One sailor, terrified, looked up at one point to see a ghostly figure charging up the deck "like a ferocious lion" in a peaked cap and blue cape.

The final moment came when a huge rogue wave

smashed the decks, picking up the captain and cracking his head against a bulwark. The captain, stunned for a moment, eventually opened his eyes and addressed his crew.

"Put her about," he moaned. "We're going back to Crouse."

That is what they did, even though the season had barely begun. The thieves replaced the now much-battered wreath back on the grave of Lajeunesse. And that, according to legend, was enough to lay to rest the ghost of the Frenchman. The *Daisy May* sailed back to Labrador and got a fair catch.

According to Norris, one solitary white china rose hung forlornly from the grave of the Frenchman into the 1940s, all that remained of that precious artifact.

"It was a beautiful wreath, that," Norris's old gentleman storyteller told her, "a beautiful, beautiful wreath."

THE LEGEND OF KITTY CASEY

Elliston

The people of Elliston, formerly known as Bird Island Cove and located on the northeast edge of the Bonavista Peninsula, are no strangers to an eerie tale. One of their most famous local legends is that of a ghostly figure named Kitty Casey or Kitty Kazzer.

Kitty Casey was the wife of Paddy Casey. They lived near Casey Gulch, around Sandy Cove. She took her own life on September 26, 1862, as her husband stood trial for stealing fish. Historian Nimshi Crewe wrote about the case in a letter dated September 28, 1964.

> "I have often heard of this tragedy," writes Crewe. "Casey, who was a tanner by trade, was either an Irishman or a native of Hr. Grace. I think he came to Bird Is. Cove as a shareman with my great-grandfather, Richard Cole. He came to be a planter on his own account, his stage being in what is still known as Casey's Gulch. He lived nearby, on the Point. His sister lived with him, and a child who married one Tom Sullivan, who lived for years as a fisherman there and, later, moved to St. John's."

Crewe learned some of the details about the fish theft from Lloyd Hicks of Elliston, who was then eighty-four years of age.

> "Lloyd has told me of an episode of Paddy going into the stage of the brothers John and Big Tom Porter after night and stealing fish," writes Crewe. "They suspected some theft and, lying in wait, caught Paddy in the act; he tried to escape by jumping over the stagehead and swimming, but they caught him and took him up to William Minty, the constable, who kept him in his kitchen all night and took him to the magistrate in Bonavista next morning."

Elliston, 2012. Photo courtesy Kenny Louie, Flickr (CC BY 2.0).

According to local stories, Kitty was so overcome and distraught by her husband's criminal deeds that she decided to commit suicide in a most dramatic fashion. The woman stabbed herself five times in the throat. Astonishingly, Kitty did not die immediately. She lingered for a time afterwards, and Crewe reports one gruesome detail of her final days: "raisins she attempted to eat came out through the cuts in her throat."

A document sent to me by Marilyn Coles-Hayley, "The Day Book," St. John's, September 26, 1862, has a long letter from Bonavista, including this paragraph about a session of the Supreme Court:

> Nearly the whole of today has been spent in the case of The Queen vs. Patrick Casey, the prisoner being found guilty. During the course of this trial, a messenger came from Bird Island Cove (where the prisoner resided) to say that his wife had just cut her throat and was in a dying state. She has since been visited by a Doctor, who says she cut herself in five places, and that there is no hope for her recovery. She is now dead. The prisoner, Patrick Casey, was sentenced to one month's imprisonment.

Because she had taken her own life she was not buried in the local cemetery, as the belief of the day held that suicides could not be buried in consecrated ground. She was instead buried outside of the church, in the droke in Sandy Cove near Tilley Farm Road. The unmarked grave was covered with rocks.

There are those who believe that poor Kitty still roams Sandy Cove looking for peace and forgiveness. People have seen a strange figure coming out of the cold night fog, a mournful figure with a haunted, lost look on her face. Some have even claimed to have seen the gashes Kitty made to her long white throat. Others say she wanders the area, missing her head entirely.

If you are visiting Elliston in the fall of the year, take care where you walk in the evening. Most people will not venture down by the beach on foggy, cool nights, especially around September 26, when the sightings of Kitty are said to become more intense.

Time your excursion to Sandy Cove appropriately.

ASTRIDE A PALE HORSE

Mount Pearl, Mattis Point, and Bay Roberts

I have come across many stories of ghost horses from all around the world. Newfoundland has its own history of ghostly steeds, and my favourite local ghost horse is the one that belonged to Lady Anne Pearl.

Lady Pearl was the wife of James Pearl, after whom Mount Pearl is named. Part of their Mount Pearl farm included grounds set aside specifically for horse racing, including a benched gallery for spectators and a rounded track. After the death of her husband in Newfoundland, Lady Pearl left for England. She was fated never to roam her estate again in her lifetime. She took up residence in London and died there childless in 1860.

Soon after her death, strange reports began to circulate around the farms and summer cottages near the Mount Pearl holdings. As the legend is told, Anne's love of horse riding was stronger than the confines of the grave. Starting shortly after Lady Pearl's death, nocturnal visitors to her former riding grounds were witness to the figure of the lady astride a phantom white horse.

If a ghost horse is good, a headless ghost horse is even

better. I came across a snippet of a story from the Port au Port Peninsula, which had been collected by students in the region and published in 1972. The students wrote:

> There was a story told of a horse with no head that could be seen along the road. When a person encountered this horse he could not pass it until the horse disappeared. This phantom horse was supposed to be big and white.

Then, much to my delight, the students wrote the following addendum:

> Another story was that a pig used to appear along the road. This pig seemed to stretch along the road as the person walked.

It is, I assure you, the only reference I have ever come across to a stretching phantom pig.

But back to the business of ghostly horses. Another intriguing yarn comes from Mattis Point. Originally known as Indian Head, the community of Mattis Point lies on Newfoundland's west coast, located near Bay St. George.

Today, the old Mattis Point cemetery is overgrown with brush and alders. Its oldest legible gravestones date to the early 1900s, bearing local names such as Alexander, Bennett, Brumsey, King, Tobin, and Young. The cemetery may be older than the early twentieth century, as it also contains several unmarked graves and many white crosses and stones with no inscriptions visible. It is possible that one of those ancient graves is associated with an old ghost story.

The story involves a team of phantom horses hauling a wooden coffin up Mattis Point Hill. A team of horses appears around the bend in the road, pulling behind them a black wooden cart. As it draws closer, an object can be seen positioned on the back of the wagon, and as it draws closer still, the object can be identified. It is a single wooden coffin draped in black cloth. Pulling its silent and sombre load, the phantom horses pass by and climb up the hill.

"Alice" grew up in Mattis Point and is one of the people who remembers hearing about the ghostly procession. "It looked like a coffin in the back of the wagon," Alice told me, but she is quick to add, "I didn't see this, of course. I only heard of the story that happened years ago."

On some occasions, ghost horses are not seen but heard.

A woman who lived near Church Hill in Bay Roberts heard something very eerie, which in her estimation led to a visit from the "Old Hag," whom you shall encounter later in this book.

"One night in July of 2013, I decided to walk to the store. On my way back home around the Cable Building area, I heard what sounded like a horse galloping sound behind me. I looked back but didn't see anything. When I got home my body felt drained and my eyes were closing, I felt that tired. So I lay down to sleep, and that night I got hagged the worst hag I had in my life."

Ever since that night, the woman has been nervous to walk down Water Street around the Cable Building at night.

"I blame those horse galloping sounds I heard."

There are many folk beliefs around horses, particularly white horses, which are often thought to be harbingers of ill fortune. Dreaming of a white horse meant a coming death, and in the New Testament, one of the Four Horsemen of the Apocalypse rides astride a white horse. There was a belief around the Torbay area that a pregnant woman should never look at a white horse. To do so, according to the tradition, was to invite problems during childbirth.

I learned of one other "bad luck" association with horses from the late George Jones, originally of Riverhead, Brigus. A man who worked on boats most of his life, latterly as a ship's engineer, Jones told me once that they would never talk about horses while at sea. To do so, he said, was to call up a storm.

CHAPTER THREE
Historical and Contemporary Legends

Once, there was a serial killer that used to go around Sunshine Park killing those who ventured onto the smaller, darker paths. The police could not find him, because he always wore yellow gloves and left no fingerprints. Eventually, the police tracked him down, and he was sent to jail.

In the years that passed, a camp started up at the park. Every year they held an annual campfire. Campers would stay there all night and either sleep in tents or in the chalet at the entrance to the park.

On the eve of the campfire, the police told the camp counsellors that they were releasing the serial killer.

"You can't do that!" said the counsellors. "There are going to be a lot of kids here, and we don't want him to do anything!"

"It will be fine," said the police. "He is a changed man."

They went ahead with the campfire, but afterwards, when they sat on the chalet stairs to do a head count, two campers were missing. So they divided up into groups and went back to the campfire area to search.

One kid got separated and in the dark tripped over something.

To his horror, he found that it was a dead body, and he hurried back to the chalet to tell everyone. When he arrived, he found that everyone else had been murdered. Sitting there was an axe, and on the axe was a yellow glove, the signature of the Sunshine Park serial killer.

— Adapted from a story told by Emma Burry as part of the Young Folklorists Program in St. John's, 2011

The Night-Time Review.
Illustration by Hermann Freihold Plüddemann, 1852.

LIGHTS IN THE FOG

NAIN, TORS COVE, HEAD OF BAY D'ESPOIR, HARBOUR BRETON, AND SANDY COVE

"It often happens that one hour is hot, the next hour is cold, then a Fogge afterwards clear, then Rain—so that it commonly falls out that you get Four or Five kinds of weather in one day."

Able Seaman Aaron Thomas wrote that about Newfoundland weather in 1794, and for anyone who has lived in or visited the province, this rings as true today as it might have in the eighteenth century. It is said that one of the foggiest places on earth is the Grand Banks, that misty meeting place of the cold northern Labrador Current and the warmer Gulf Stream from the south. On average, Newfoundland and Labrador's capital city gets about 121 days per year with fog, which is not nearly as bad as Argentia, which has been known to receive over 200 days a year of fog. So it is not strange at all that many local myths and legends revolve around fog, bad weather, and means of predicting weather changes.

While most of the stories presented to this point have been legends, stories which were perceived as being based in truth in the historical period, the next story is more cosmological in nature. It could be defined as an "etiological" myth. Etiological myths are origin or creation stories, which describe how things around us came into being. In this instance, it is one from Labrador which lays out the story of how fog came to be.

Miller's Passage, Connaigre Peninsula, no date. Photo PF-328.117, courtesy Resettlement Photographs, Maritime History Archive.

The indigenous peoples of this province dealt with fog for centuries before the Europeans showed up, and it is no wonder that local myths evolved around that mysterious, misty stuff. In 2008, Dr. Hans Rollmann of Memorial University wrote an article in Newfoundland and Labrador Studies documenting a fog-related story written by Reverend Albert Martin in a 1901 Moravian magazine. Martin had lived in Labrador from 1888 until 1923 and had served as the Moravian superintendent of Labrador. Martin heard the story in Labrador, though there are versions of the story found across the Arctic.

"Once, a man went into the forest to get firewood," writes

Martin. "While he was working in the forest, he was attacked by a black bear who wounded him badly, so that the man fell to the ground as if dead. The bear sniffed him to determine whether he was still alive, but the man held his breath, so that the bear believed the man to be dead and put him on his back to carry him off into his cave."

Eventually, the man escaped and ran away from the bear. The bear gave chase and found the hunted man standing on the other side of a river.

"How have you been able to cross the river?" the bear asked the man.

"I drank it all up," the man answered.

"The bear immediately started to do the same," says Martin. "He drank and drank and drank, until he burst. Then, for the first time, thick fog covered the land."

All that fog shrouding the coasts and bays of Newfoundland and Labrador comes with its own attendant folklore. Weather lights are a truly persistent bit of Newfoundland weather lore, and stories of strange lights associated with bad or "dirty" weather can be found in every corner of the province. According to the *Dictionary of Newfoundland English*, a weather light is a gleam or flicker of light at sea thought to presage a storm.

The *Dictionary* gives a few examples of how the phrase is used. P. Delaney of Tors Cove is quoted as saying, "when you can see [weather] lights on the salt water at night, it is a sign of a storm ahead," while E. Cokes of Head of Bay D'Espoir is quoted as reporting that "weather lights in the riggings of a schooner is the sign of a storm coming. The lights start at the bottom of the riggings and move gradually up to the top where they disappear."

Another community home to these lights is Harbour Breton, on the south coast of the island. Doug Wells, a native of Harbour Breton, sent me a series of articles on local culture, thinking the ones concerned with strange phenomena might be of interest to me.

"I had my students write on local cultural and historical events," explains Wells. "With a folklore background, I also encouraged students to write articles on folklore-related practices. The articles are folklore and folklife-related and represent Harbour Breton and some nearby resettled communities. Over the years of teaching Cultural Heritage 1200, students wrote approximately 150 stories."

One of Wells's students was Ryan Lambert, of King Academy, who wrote on the local tradition of what he termed "dirty weather lights." Lambert documents two examples of this luminescent occurrence from the communities of Miller's Passage and Harbour Breton.

"In Miller's Passage the dirty weather light would float slowly in through the harbour, through the tickle," says Lambert, "and as it reached Shoal Cove it would turn around, float out through the tickle, out the harbour and vanish. The next day, as usual, the residents would get wind and rain—a disappointing day for fishermen. People noticed that the dirty weather light would follow the same path almost all the time. It was a frightening experience at first, but people soon grew accustomed to it and expected bad weather to follow."

A similar weather light was also seen in Harbour Breton.

"It would be seen mostly by people living on the north side," writes Lambert. "The dirty weather light would float in over Deadman's Cove Road and travel slowly as far as the present town garage. It would then stop, turn around, and head toward Deadman's Cove again and then vanish. And again, probably as in all dirty weather light sightings, the weather would soon turn bad."

Lambert also references a man by the name of Josiah Bullen, of Harbour Breton, who could vividly remember seeing the dirty weather light, both as a boy and as a married man.

"Mr. Bullen describes it as floating just above the ground as bright as a good-sized flashlight," says Lambert. "Some members of Mr. Bullen's family would be scared of the light, especially his wife, Meta, after she moved to Harbour Breton from Little Bay West in the early 1940s."

Bullen noted that once houses were built in the area, the light was never seen again.

"He says that you could expect to see the dirty weather light when there was a bad-weather-look in the sky," says Lambert, "and, most generally, the weather would not be fit for anything after the light was seen."

These south coast examples are similar to stories from many places across the province. One intriguing variant, with some very specific details, comes from the community of Sandy Cove, in Bonavista Bay, not far from Eastport. One local woman told her daughter Mary about seeing a weather light in the cove, and I gave Mary a call to talk about her mother's stories.

"She called it a weather light because bad weather followed," says Mary. "My mother wasn't a superstitious person. She wasn't a person who believed in all of this stuff. She went to every possible extent to keep us from believing it. But she did tell us about that, and she said that she saw it. She had no other choice but to believe it.

"There is a real nice sandy beach there," describes Mary. "It is a big beach, a bit curved, with a high bank at the top. When you stand on that bank you see down the bay."

According to Mary's mother, it was up through there that the light would come.

"The light would come up through the bay, up and up, and it would come to the bank," says Mary. "I'm assuming she meant it came up on the bank. And then that would be it, it wouldn't come any farther than that. That meant that the next day they were likely to get bad weather.

"I was talking to my sister a few days ago, and I said to her, 'Do you remember Mom telling you about this?' 'Oh yes, Mom called it the weather light.' And she did, she could remember our mother telling her about it as well."

Mary's grandfather had been a sea captain, and she surmises that a belief in things like the weather light was part of the family's seafaring culture.

"Weather was very important to them at that time," she says, "especially when you didn't have anyone telling you every evening what it was going to be like tomorrow. I guess that anything that they could use for signs of weather, they used it. That probably was one, this particular light that used to come up."

Another local curiosity that Mary remembers her mother talking about was the similarly themed "weather axe"—a phantom axe that people heard on the eve before the arrival of bad weather.

"You'd wake up in the middle of the night sometimes when it was very still and you could hear it," says Mary. "There were woods on the back of our house, and you could hear somebody chopping wood—chop, chop, chop.

My mother used to talk about that as well, the weather axe."

Weather lights seem to be something common in many fogbound Newfoundland and Labrador communities, but Sandy Cove boasts the first weather axe story to swing my way.

THE HAUNTED TRESTLE REVISITED

Clarke's Beach

The American folklorist Robert A. Georges once wrote that a legend is "believed to be true by some, false by others, and both or neither by most." It is a definition I would agree with, and Newfoundland is full of examples. Almost every town has a story which is partly true and partly not. As a collector and lover of stories, they are my favourite kind. I think everyone has a spot in his heart for a story which, though fantastic, might possibly be true.

What I love more than hearing a local legend is hearing a legend that has multiple versions. Sometimes these are migratory legends which crop up in different forms in different communities. Sometimes, however, legends are tied to a very specific place and are largely unknown outside of their home communities.

Clarke's Beach has one of these legends, which I initially wrote up in my book *Haunted Shores.* Around 1984, three girls were out late one night, walking along the abandoned railway line that cuts through Clarke's Beach. The girls were walking from Wilsonville Avenue along the track toward an old railway trestle over North River.

As the three girls drew closer to the river, they could see a fourth girl sitting on the edge of the trestle, drying her hair with a towel. Drawing closer still, they could see that the girl was dressed in an old-fashioned bathing suit. The bather paid no attention to the threesome, and it was not until they stepped onto the wooden beams of the trestle itself that the mysterious figure lowered her towel and turned to look straight at them.

The old railway trestle between Clarke's Beach and North River, May 2017. Photo by Dale Jarvis.

The threesome stopped dead in their tracks. The girl gazed upon them, her eyes glowing with a brilliant red light, shining strong in the moonlight. The creature's gaze was enough to send the three young girls screaming in terror back to the relative safety of Clarke's Beach.

Theirs was not the first sighting of the midnight bathing beauty. In conversation with an elderly man who lived on

Wilsonville Avenue, he learned that the form was the spectre of a local girl. The girl had arranged to meet her sweetheart for a late-night rendezvous and swim. When he did not arrive, she took to the waters. Then, tragedy: the bathing beauty slipped beneath the silent waves and drowned alone in the darkness.

Apparently, the girl's ghost returned from the netherworld to haunt the spot of her demise, doomed to spend the sweet hereafter waiting by the railway line for a love fated never to arrive.

It is a great story. It was published, and then it faded into the background of my memory.

A decade later, folklorist Lisa Wilson and I started a project in co-operation with the Bay Roberts Cultural Foundation to document the folklore, legends, traditional cures, fairy stories, and folk beliefs of Bay Roberts and surrounding area. Part of the collection work involved the students of teacher Kimberley Welsh at Ascension Collegiate. Students were encouraged to go home, learn traditional stories from family and neighbours, and then report back.

I was delighted when two of those students returned with variants of the Clarke's Beach trestle story. One student, Brittany Corbett, shared a fairly succinct version.

"The trestle in North River was known to be haunted," wrote Corbett. "In the night you should stay away because there was a girl killed on it. She haunts the trestle and she will try and kill you."

Another student, Josh Russell, offered up a slightly longer version. He wrote,

"At Clarke's Beach Pond where the metal bridge is, there is a hill that leads into a pond, and behind is a forest where dirt bikes and quads go past. Years ago a lady was knelt down by the pond washing her old clothes, because back then there was no washing machines to clean your clothes like there is today. She lost balance and fell into the pond, and because she didn't know how to swim, she drowned. It is said that if you go on the bridge where she drowned, you can see her ghost with red eyes on the hill washing clothes."

While both these are different from the version I wrote up in 2004, there are intriguing similarities, particularly in Russell's telling of the story. The glowing red eyes and the drowning are intact. One could even draw a parallel between the towel in the early version and the washing in the more recent one.

Today, the abandoned train trestle remains to cross the river, even though the tracks themselves have long since vanished. Intriguingly, the glowing-eyed spectre is not the only ghost to have been reported in that vicinity.

One fine evening in 1907, a Clarke's Beach man decided to take a stroll along the railway track. As he did, he heard a familiar sound. He turned, and there in the distance was a steam locomotive, chugging toward him.

The train drew closer and showed no sign of slowing down to stop at the station. He watched as it moved closer and felt the vibration of the great engine shaking the earth as it roared past. From where he stood, he could see several people on board, staring out through the windows. He raised his walking stick in greeting, but no one waved back, the passengers' eyes fixed on something in the distance.

Puzzled, he decided he would stop in at the railway station and ask about the train that had just gone through. The station was empty except for the ticket agent.

"No train has passed through here," said the agent.

The agent checked the timetables and found that a train had not been scheduled, nor was one expected. News of the phantom train was telegraphed up along the line, but no train arrived at the station in Bay Roberts. The story was made known in the community, and others corroborated his story. They too had seen the strange train. However, no explanation was ever found. The railway hands who worked that section of the line were somewhat spooked by the story and from that point on were always nervous about meeting the ghostly engine somewhere on the tracks.

Ghostly trains are a recurring theme in contemporary legends, and the locomotive itself is an example of folk literature motif E535.4—"Phantom railway train." The Clarke's Beach example may not be the only phantom train in the province. While he remained vague on specific locations, Newfoundland writer P. J. Kinsella noted in 1910 that, "there is a phantom train that runs along near a certain station, and the villagers, who often hear its weird whistle, have much reason to entertain a strange superstition in connection with its nightly progress."

While the phantom locomotive story is probably an example of a legend with variants found around the world, what is curious about the Clarke's Beach trestle is that it seems to be a focal point for local supernatural stories. The adjacent Clarke's Beach Salvation Army Cemetery, incidentally, is said to be haunted by the ghost of a man wearing a top hat. Though I have looked more than once, I have never caught sight of this rather debonair ghost.

HARK! PHANTOM DRUMMERS AND PIPERS

Marysvale, Brigus, Bay Roberts, and Swift Current

Imagine a calm night, with only a little wind moving the clouds overhead. Everything is quiet, but then, out of the stillness, you hear a noise. Listen very carefully. At first, it sounds like a distant tapping, but as it draws closer, you realize it is the sound of a drum, a tattoo beaten out with military precision. But who would be playing a drum there, in the middle of the night? If you are in the right spot, at the right time, it might be a ghostly drummer.

The *Feildian* was the magazine of Bishop Feild College, a Church of England academy for boys. The magazine ran from 1893 to 1960 and was created to foster school feeling and to chronicle College affairs. It was the first publication of its kind on the island and included news, letters, sports, and reports from school alumni.

In a 1905 article entitled "What About Ghosts?" a writer identified only as "H." claimed to have put to rest a story about a ghost. Sadly, the mysterious author did not mention the location of the ghost story, only that it was at the mouth of a bay, "on the bank of a river close to a mountain gorge containing a lagoon."

"The lagoon was reported to be haunted by a deserter from a French warship," writes H., "who had died in a fisherman's cottage in the bay, after several years spent in the woods, in fear of recapture. He had been a drummer on the ship, and he swore to the woman who had nursed him on his deathbed that he would haunt the lagoon, a weird and lonely spot. For years his drum was heard beating at certain periods, as his spirit marched through the woods, and many a time parties visiting the place fled in terror from its supernatural roll."

One evening, the author was sitting in the twilight after supper, camped on the reportedly haunted spot.

An English drummer boy. Illustration by George W. Joy, 1902.

"My guide was at the brook washing up, and I was placidly smoking, seated on a stone," writes H., "with my back against a telegraph pole, the line of which ran through this country for many miles. Suddenly in the dreamy silence broke the beating of a drum, and my man came running back with a scared face. I at once recognized the sound, but could see no ghost, so . . . I kept my head and began to look for the spectre.

"I soon noticed that angry gusts of wind were coming down through the gorge," he notes, "and as these passed, the drum rolled out, I observed a tremor in the telegraph pole. This gave me a clue, and immediately afterwards I saw the ghost in the wire. In short, the drum was the wind playing on a mile of telegraph wire, and reverberating in the cliffs as the 'spouts' came down the gorge from the North East."

The ghost story that H. wanted to debunk may have been part of a regionally famous set of ghost stories clustered in one very particular geographic area: a section of Conception Bay defined by Marysvale to the south and Bay Roberts to the north.

If you turn off that stretch of the old Conception Bay highway and explore the community of Marysvale, formerly known as Turk's Gut, you will find the Turk's Gut Heritage House at the end of the road toward the water. The building is home to the Turk's Gut Heritage Committee, where Mrs. Bride Power has been working hard to preserve the oral history and folklore of the community. It was through Bride that I tracked down the details of the Turk's Gut version of the phantom drummer.

Local folklore maintains that the drummer lived in Turk's Gut in the early part of the 1800s. Exactly where he came from is something of a mystery. Some believe that the drummer was a prisoner of war, while others hold that he arrived as a stowaway on a sailing ship. No one in Turk's Gut knew where the man had come from, nor did they know his true name. The man himself could offer little assistance, for he seemed to know just as little about his own identity. The man had some sort of amnesia, and it was thought by the local people that he had suffered some sort of memory loss, perhaps due to a war injury.

While the stranger could not remember his name or where he was born, he did retain one impressive skill. He did remember how to play the drum, and so was nicknamed "The Drummer" by the local residents.

The drummer was taken in and shown great courtesy by a local family, the Simmses. After living in Turk's Gut for many years, the drummer passed away. The Simms family buried the man on their property and laid a flat rock over his grave to mark his final resting spot. That rock was said to be located about seventy-five feet from where the Turk's Gut Heritage House stands now.

Eternal rest, however, seemed to elude the drummer. Long after his death, his ghost could be heard playing an invisible drum. Before long, stories began to spread that when people in the drummer's adopted home passed away, the drummer could be heard for miles around.

The noise of the drummer was heard only during the night when all was quiet. It was also rumoured that on the eve of a local person's death the drummer could be heard playing the drums under the windowsill of the person who was fated to die.

In 1956, a different version of the legend was written down by a man named Don Morris, who published the article in a magazine titled *Here in Newfoundland.* Morris claimed to have learned the story from Leo English, a curator at the Newfoundland Museum.

Morris's version placed the recurring haunting in Brigus and concerned a phantom drummer said to play at funerals. The Brigus variant claimed that an English drummer had once made a promise to an old Brigus settler that the musician would drum the old man to his grave, and that he would also drum at the funerals of all his direct descendants. Soon after, the old man died. Morris writes,

> And true to his word, the drummer followed the coffin to the grave beating solemnly on his drum. He performed

> the same ritual for other direct descendants . . . and then the drummer, by this time an old man himself, passed on to his eternal reward. But mysteriously the drumming went on . . . and is going on. . . . And since then in Brigus, whenever a direct descendant of the drummer's benefactor dies, the beating of a drum can be heard while the funeral procession is en route to the graveyard.

The northern edge of the drummer's Conception Bay territory seems to be Bay Roberts. Folklorist Lisa Wilson collected one short version of a phantom drummer story in 2013 from Audrey Sparkes, of Bay Roberts.

"There used to be the front road school and we went up to our W.A. [Women's Auxiliary] meeting, myself and two other ladies. See, I had just moved. I wasn't familiar with anything. We were walking home and there's a rock there . . . and it was called the Drummer's Rock. And we're walking home and it is a wild night, and this noise, and one said to the other, 'The drummer is playing on the rock tonight.' I was ready to fly but I just walked on with them."

The exact location of Drummer's Rock seems hard to pin down, though the *Bay Roberts Guardian* newspaper noted, on Friday, August 10, 1928, the August 7 death of Robert C. Bradbury "aged 80 years, who was born at Drummer's Rock, French's Cove, July 12th, 1848." This notation would seem to place the rock at the northeastern end of Bay Roberts.

I was told that the best person to talk to about the location and legend of Drummer's Rock would be Sandra Roach. Roach is the general manager of the Bay Roberts Cultural Foundation, and one of the people responsible for keeping the Drummer's Rock story alive.

Her version of the story came from her husband, Harry's, mother, Emmie May (Crane) Roach. Emmie died in August 2016, at the age of ninety-six. She had grown up in the area around Crane's Hill in Bay Roberts East, and as Emmie's grandfather lived on Crane's Hill Road, it is possible that the hill is named after her branch of the Crane family.

The path to the Drummer's Rock, Bay Roberts, May 2017.
Photo by Dale Jarvis.

According to Emmie's story, many years ago, British warships patrolling for enemy vessels occasionally anchored in Bay Roberts harbour, off French's Cove. On board one of these ships there was a young seaman who served as their drummer. His duty was to play reveille, to call the sailors for meals, or to call them to arms if they were approached by an enemy ship. This boy decided he did not want the life of a drummer, and he jumped ship. He either swam or rowed ashore in French's Cove and ran up the path which locals called the Front Road.

"When the soldiers on board discovered that he was gone, of course they came looking for him," describes Roach. "When they did find him, he was hiding behind a large boulder which became known as Drummer's Rock. When they found him, they flogged him to death with a cat-o'-nine-tails."

The cat-o'-nine-tails is a type of whip and was described in a 1911 criminology journal in this way:

> The cat as now in use consists of nine cords attached to a handle. At the extremity of each cord are three or four knots. The prisoner is tied to a sort of frame, the arms above the head. A prison guard wields the cat with all his force so that the knots strike the prisoner between the shoulders. . . . It is rare that the flesh is not so torn that permanent scars are carried by the prisoner.

It was a common naval punishment in the era of naval exploration, and David D. Porter, admiral of the United States Navy, wrote this about the naval use of the cat-o'-nine-tails in 1890:

> On my first acquaintance with the navy, in 1823, there was but one kind of punishment for the men in vogue on shipboard. That was by the use of the cat-o'-nine-tails, a relic of barbarism handed down from the time of good Queen Bess, who prided herself on the navy which repulsed the "Invincible Armada" of ten times its own strength. Under the discipline of early times, of which the press gang and the "cats" were such potent factors, the British navy captured or destroyed nearly everything opposed to it. Whip-

> ping was considered the best means of disciplining a crew, whereas, in fact, it made mere brutes of the sailors, who in those days had perhaps scarcely sentiment enough in them to appreciate the degradation to which they were subjected. . . . It is strange, but true, that many old seamen who were partial to the service for the sake of the grog, which they received three times a day, were equally opposed to the abolition of the "cat." The "cat," they argued, was a wholesome terror to worthless loafers about decks, and the only means of making them do their duty.

And so, whipped he was, our drummer boy, and the unfortunate lad perished from his wounds. The folklore of Bay Roberts maintains that his tortured soul returned to drum near the rock where he expired.

"Emmie's mother used to say to her, 'don't go near that rock,' because the legend has it the people over time would hear a drum being played near that rock," says Roach. "She was told to stay away from it. Another lady said that people used to see a light coming up the path in the night toward Drummer's Rock, and they would hear someone crying."

In addition to Drummer's Rock in Bay Roberts, there is also a shoal called Drummer's Rock near Harbour Grace, and, slightly more farther afield, a Drummer's Pond on the Fox Harbour Road between Fox Harbour and Dunville, near Placentia. The jury is still out on whether either of those places is haunted.

The ghostly drummer legend is related to other local legends about ghostly pipers. Indeed, ghostly musicians are so well-represented in supernatural literature that folklorists have assigned the trope its own number—folk literature motif E402.1.13, "Invisible ghost plays musical instrument." Dover Castle, in Dover, Kent, England, is said to be the eternal home of a headless drummer boy in Napoleonic era costume who haunts the castle, for example.

The most famous Newfoundland example of the ghostly piper legend explains the name behind Piper's Hole, near Swift Current on the Burin Peninsula, a story I documented in my book *Haunted Shores.* There, a ghostly piper has been playing his instrument for centuries.

Don Ryan described the legend thusly in 1957:

> Legend has it that a squad of French soldiers, at the time when the French had set up their capital at Placentia, reconnoitred the inland reaches of the bay and found a rapidly flowing stream at the bottom of its northernmost reach. While exploring this river they came in contact with the English who were lying in wait for them and a skirmish took place. One Frenchman was killed, but for some unknown reason his spirit still lingered in the valley. Years later, villagers would hear this spirit piping mournful notes, but only in the late evening and on the wings of a northeast wind would the melancholy air reach the ears of the villages. For this reason they said that the valley, extending from Larkin's Hill, was haunted by this phantom piper. Hence, they called the valley Piper's Hole and the stream which flowed between the hills, Piper's Hole River.

A 1992 edition of the Newfoundland magazine *Decks Awash* noted that the "story is told of the crowd of deer hunters who actually danced to the sound of the pipes."

In the years since the publication of *Haunted Shores*, I have tracked down several other versions of the legend. One version, printed in 1901, tells of two deserters from the Royal Navy named Dick Huntley and Ned Fitzgerald. The two men encountered the sound of a piper near Rattling Brook, at the spot where it entered Piper's Creek, on a fine evening in the month of September 1750.

> That night they camped on an island in the lagoon and waited anxiously for a repetition of the same strange programme to which they had listened on the previous night. Sometime after midnight: the strange music again rang out on the clear night air, and apparently at no great distance. . . . They entered the boat and pulled in the direction of the music. On turning a point they came upon a strange scene. Seated on a huge boulder, the bright rays of the moon glistening on his snow-white hair and beard, and with his attenuated fingers clasping the chanter of his instrument, sat the piper. As the boat glided toward him, he finished off with a shrill burst of music, and to their horror they saw him plunge beneath the waves and disappear. For some time they remained as if spellbound, and as the boat was touching the shore they jumped out and made a thorough search but could find no clue to the mystery.

According to some, the phantom musician was a piper in the French army in the eighteenth century. In one version of the legend, the French and English clashed in battle at Garden Cove. Supposedly, the spirit of the French soldier lingers in the river valley, mournfully playing a tune. In other versions from the same area, the musician was a Scottish bagpiper, killed in a hunting accident by an Englishman.

What makes the entire set of stories complicated, but which also links them to the phantom drummer stories of Conception Bay, is that in at least one early version of the Piper's Hole legend, the ghost plays both the pipes and a drum.

In a 1912 article called "Lore of Placentia Bay," Richard S. Dahl wrote that the ghost had been a fifer and drummer in the army, a man named Kelly who confessed on his deathbed to being a murderer.

> Kelly died and then began the nightly music that gave the inlet its name. On many nights the thundering roll of a mighty drum would be heard patrolling up and down the valley, or the shrieking whistle of a giant fife would be heard above the roar of the storm. And even in peaceful weather the drummer might pursue a belated traveller. The settlers became unnerved, and the settlement disappeared. When I heard the story I jotted it down and thought no more about it. When last fall I was anchored at Indian Cove, at the mouth of Piper's Hole, we had wind and tide against us and would not attempt to negotiate the sandbanks, twists and turns of Piper's Hole under such conditions. The night was light and about ten o'clock out comes a craft, spite sandbanks and tides, with every sail set and every man on deck. They had been loading firewood at dusk, at the mouth of Kelly's Brook, when the drummer had come thundering down the ravine

> and the seven stalwart men had fled, hoisted the anchor, and set sail —in the year of our Lord 1911.

So, whether the legend is truly about a piper, a drummer, or some other type of ghostly musician, there is something about it that keeps people coming back to the story. Indeed, Sandra Roach and the Bay Roberts Cultural Foundation have taken the old legend and have updated it for the modern tourism age, incorporating the story into various cultural programs, including their popular "Toutons & Tunes" tour on the Heritage Walking Trail.

"We have a young boy run up the path, all out of breath, with his shirttail out, and a soldier chasing him with the cat-o'-nine-tails in his hand," describes Roach. "He says to the crowd, 'I was on that ship anchored out in the harbour,' and we made up a little bit that he stole some bread. The soldier comes looking for him, then he runs off and you hear the cat-o'-nine-tails off in the distance, and him crying. Then we tell the story of how that happened, and how he was killed. We do it on the trail, near the old United Church School which was there on the Front Road. There is a rock foundation there where the school was. So we start there, about halfway down toward Bishop's Beach."

Roach also tells the story of Drummer's Rock as part of the Bay Roberts Cultural Foundation's show "The Haunting."

"As people gather around I tell them all about the ships in the harbour, and how the boy came ashore," she tells me. "We had a summer student with a little snare drum, and he used to sit over by the church, and as soon as I stopped telling my story he'd do a little 'tap-tap-tap' on the drum.

"People loved it."

MYSTERIOUS NORSEMEN

L'Anse aux Meadows, Bay de L'Eau, Harbour Mille, and Muddy Cove

I have been a fan of Viking tales and Norse mythology since I was very young. I still have my well-thumbed copy of the children's book *Eric: A Tale of a Red-Tempered Viking* by Susan McDonald Bond, originally published in 1968. It tells the tale of Erik the Red, and his son Leif the Lucky, who went on to discover Vinland.

That early love of the old Norse stories has stayed with me. A return trip to the L'Anse aux Meadows National Historic Site of Canada and the nearby Norstead Viking Village enticed me to dig out my copy of the Vinland Sagas, searching for a half-remembered ghost story.

The town of L'Anse aux Meadows is home to the first-discovered European settlement in the New World. The remains at the Parks Canada site, discovered by archaeologists Helge and Anne Stine Ingstad, were declared a UNESCO World Heritage Site in 1978. While we may never know if Leif the Lucky himself walked the shores at L'Anse aux Meadows, we know with certainty that his countrymen did.

In addition to Leif, Erik the Red had three other children: a daughter, Freydis, and two additional sons, Thorvald and Thorstein. Unfortunately for the two other sons, they were not quite as lucky as their brother. Thorvald died and was buried somewhere in Vinland. He was shot in the armpit with an arrow fired at him by an angry Skraeling, one of Vinland's aboriginal inhabitants, after Thorvald and his men had captured three Skraeling boats and killed their owners.

We saw the shore. Illustration by Mary Hallock Foote, 1877.

When Thorstein heard of his brother's death, he was determined to sail to Vinland and bring back Thorvald's body. He took twenty-five men, and his wife, Gudrid, along. But early that winter, disease broke out among the crew, eventually spreading to Thorstein himself. He died and was greatly mourned by Gudrid.

Things then took a turn toward the supernatural. What follows is the earliest-known European ghost story in North America. Gudrid was being consoled by one of the crew when the body of Thorstein Eiriksson sat up on the bench where he had been laid out.

"Where is Gudrid?" he asked.

His wife, perhaps rightfully terrified at this, said nothing. Three times the corpse spoke, asking for his wife. Three times she said nothing. One of the crew members, also named Thorstein, spoke up instead.

"What is it you want, namesake?" asked the second Thorstein.

At this the corpse spoke again, saying that he was anxious to reveal to Gudrid her destiny. He went on, prophesying that his wife would have a bountiful future, that she would remarry, have children, outlive her second husband, go on pilgrimage to Rome, return to Iceland, build a church, become a nun, and die there in her old age. As far as life predictions go, it is not a bad one, really.

Having said his bit, the corpse fell back onto the bench. The Vikings packed him up and sailed with him back to Eiriksfjord, Greenland, the town his father had established. Thorstein was buried there, and presumably did not speak again.

While Thorstein Eiriksson may have been the first Viking ghost in Newfoundland, he was definitely not the last. One Halloween, I sat down at a St. John's coffee shop with Colin, who had a treasure trove of ghost stories from Harbour Mille and Grand Bank, the far side of the province from L'Anse aux Meadows. His family was one of the founding families of Harbour Mille, and he was full of stories about various members coming back from the dead to say hello or show displeasure about the actions of the living.

Today, Harbour Mille is a small fishing village of around 200 people in Fortune Bay, about twenty-six kilometres off the Burin Peninsula Highway. The town sits on an isthmus, and hills rise, saddle-like, to the west and the east. It has both a sheltered harbour at the north and a beach to the south.

Across the bay to the northwest is the now-abandoned community of Bay de L'Eau. Though separated by five or six kilometres of open water, the two communities are linked by a rather intriguing ghost story. Colin learned the Bay de L'Eau half of the ghost story from a friend, David, who also has roots in the Harbour Mille area.

As the legend goes, there was a group of fishermen in a schooner sailing into Bay de L'Eau. As they came close to land, they saw what they later described as a Viking ship coming out of the bay.

"The description that the sailors gave afterwards was very much like a Viking longship," says Colin. "The men were wearing fur pelts and of course speaking a language which they didn't understand."

The two companies parted ways, and the longship vanished from sight.

"When David heard the story, he thought 'they're describing a Viking ship, with Vikings on it,'" says Colin. "This is rather interesting, because this ties into a story from Harbour Mille with my dear Aunt Sarah."

Aunt Sarah was Colin's great-grandfather's sister-in-law, who lived in Harbour Mille in the late 1800s. Aunt Sarah was the source of the second half of the ghost story, passed down to Colin from his father and grandfather.

"She heard this ruckus, and she thought there was some kind of a social or whatever going on in the Orange Lodge," recalls Colin. "This was at night. She looked out through her bedroom window, the second storey, and she said these men came in on a barge, into the harbour, got to the shore, lifted the barge up on their shoulders, and then walked out over the hills with the barge. So I'm wondering if this barge isn't the same ship."

Aunt Sarah heard the men talking but couldn't understand them as it was a "foreign tongue."

"That would have happened in the mid to late 1800s," he adds. "'Barge' is not a word which we would have ever really used, so I don't know where she got the word 'barge.'"

His interpretation is that Aunt Sarah used the word "barge" to describe an unfamiliar long, flat boat.

The story of the men picking up the "barge" and carrying it across the hills is equally intriguing. Viking longships were constructed to be both light and strong; the crew of a small one could quite easily take down the mast, overturn the craft, and portage it over land to the next fjord or bay if needed. It has been argued that this capability added to the legendary suddenness and speed of Norse raiders.

L'Anse aux Meadows itself is also home to a ghost Viking ship, and there are several different versions of the legend. One local boy named Conor wrote up the story as it had been told to him by his great-grandmother, Mamie Taylor, who grew up in L'Anse aux Meadows. According to her version, the haunting would take place every year on the same night. On the evening of July 1, fishermen would hear the ghostly sounds of voices speaking in foreign tongues, the rattling of pots and pans, the rowing of oars, and the noise of footsteps on the shore.

Other popular versions of the story have the haunting occur once every thirty years in August. This rendition got a boost in 2006 when it was included in the popular Canadian paranormal television program *Creepy Canada*.

A fisherman was working late in his stage when he heard a strange noise. First, he heard the sound of oars hitting the water, and then he heard the sound of a horn. He looked out the door of his stage and saw a strange vessel being rowed toward the shore: a long, narrow open boat with one central mast and a single striped sail. Other versions have two teenaged boys witnessing a similar encounter with a long ship with a row of oars on each side heading toward land.

Local storytellers maintain that thirty years after these initial reports, a fisherman on the water encountered the same ghost ship. He had stayed out on the water later than other fishermen, but as the skies turned gloomy, he headed for the safety of the harbour. It was then that he too heard a noise in the water, like the sound of men rowing. He looked up just in time to see a great Viking ship bearing down on him. At the last moment, he heard the sound of a great trumpet blowing a battle call before the ship vanished into thin air.

Authors Maureen Wood and Ron Kolek offer up yet another version of the tale, though their story starts in Reykjavik, Iceland. On June 3, 1981, two American tourists saw two

Viking longships, with a tall man with a long beard standing at the prow of one. When they told a local what they had seen, they were informed that they had been lucky enough to spot Iceland's spectral longboats, which appeared annually on the same day. The authors go on to state that, "On June 23 each year, Viking longboats are supposed to appear off the coast of L'Anse aux Meadows, Newfoundland—twenty days after they are seen in Iceland."

There is one other curious figure in L'Anse aux Meadows that may have a Viking connection, "The Brown Man of Muddy Cove." To get a local's perspective on the Brown Man, I called up businesswoman and author Gina Noordhof, who is the owner of the Valhalla Lodge and Norseman Restaurant in L'Anse aux Meadows, and a fifth-generation resident of the area.

"It may have been a way of the locals ensuring that kids were home before dark," Noordhof tells me. "They would say that the Brown Man was a man dressed all in brown clothing. Once, a man with his dog team and komatik were going for a load of wood, and though he was trying to move, he couldn't. The Brown Man was holding the komatik, you see, preventing it from moving. A lot of people would tell these tales about the Brown Man of Muddy Cove, and I think that was a Viking story. The way that some people would tell it, it seems like it was a description of a Viking. They told those tales long before the Ingstads knew anything about the archaeological site."

Researcher Kathleen Tucker collected several Brown Man stories as part of an oral history project she undertook for St. Anthony Basin Resources Inc. in 2014. She compiled those stories in a publication called *Folklore: Ghostly Tales, Su-*

perstitions and Local Traditions & Customs. Several of the people that Tucker interviewed knew versions of Noordhof's story. One of Tucker's informants was a man by the name of Winston Colbourne, who named the gentleman who had run up against the Brown Man as Uncle George Decker. As Colbourne told Tucker:

"The komatik got stuck fair in the path, though the path was smooth as could be. He was singing out to the dogs to go ahead; the dogs were rising up in their traces; but no sir, they couldn't move the komatik. Anyway, Uncle George was at it that long that Uncle Jack Hedderson over in Hay Cove took notice; he could hear the oaths coming out of him."

Uncle Jack decided to investigate, and though he could see the Brown Man, Uncle George could not. By the time Uncle Jack got close, the Brown Man had disappeared. He asked Uncle George about the stranger with whom he had been arguing.

"I was swearing on the dogs because I was stuck here," said Decker.

Uncle Jack replied, "There was a man, right in front of your dogs, and your komatik never busted clear until that man moved away."

There is a debate in the area over who the Brown Man might be. Some say he dressed in buckskins; others say he dressed in a brown suit. Noordhof thinks he was a Viking ghost; others think he may have been a Beothuk or one of those angry Skraelings who shot Thorvald Eiriksson a millennium ago. Some say he has not been seen in years, ever since his favourite seat—a chair-shaped rock—was covered over when the modern road went through in 1966.

Today it is hard to say how many of the various L'Anse

aux Meadows legends are "traditional" and how many have been embellished over the years or influenced by stories told in print and television. The numerous tales are clearly related, though they differ on details.

As for the ghostly Viking longship, debate continues on whether the haunting occurs in June, July, or August. If you are visiting the Great Northern Peninsula next summer, keep your ears open for the sound of those phantom oars hitting the water, and your eyes peeled for a glimpse of the elusive Brown Man of Muddy Cove.

RED EYES AND ROD STEWART

Glovertown

Looming just off Angle Brook Road in Glovertown is the impressive concrete ruin of an old pulp and paper mill. It is also the site of a sinister local urban legend about a mysterious spirit known as "Red Eyes."

The mill had been expected to open in 1922, but the owners, Terra Nova Sulphite Company, ran into financial problems. Their Norwegian investors had money issues at home, and they were refused a loan guarantee by the Newfoundland Government. Construction ground to a halt. In the fall of 1923, the property was purchased by Anglo-Newfoundland Development Company. The AND Company sent 1,300 cords of cut wood to the mill to test its operation and decided that the mill was too small for their needs. The mill's machines and equipment were dismantled and shipped to Bishop's Falls and Grand Falls, and today the mill still stands in its incomplete state, almost untouched since the 1920s.

For locals, it was a creepy spot, tall and still, empty, and dark even in the daylight. "The Plant" became an after-hours hangout for teenagers. By the 1950s, stories began to circulate that someone had died during the mill's construction. One rumour spread that a worker had fallen into a vat of lead, a great gruesome detail for an urban legend in the making.

David Saunders works with Parks Canada at nearby Terra Nova National Park. A mutual friend connected us, suggesting that he might know something about the legend. I got in touch with Saunders, and while he was unaware of the modern version of the Red Eyes legend, he told me a story he had learned in the mid-1980s.

The Terra Nova Sulphite Mill under construction, circa 1922.
Photo courtesy Grand Falls–Windsor Heritage Society.

"We were hanging out in the Old Mill area; I'm saying area because this story happened about a half-mile in the road from the mill at a gravel pit. A friend of mine had been 'parking' in his car, let's just say his windows were steamed up, when he heard something scraping/scratching beneath his car. He cautiously lowered his window but saw nothing around the vehicle. However, to his astonishment, there was a figure standing on a large pile of sand about a hundred feet away. I remember him saying the character had his mouth open as if he were screaming, but he didn't make a sound, and yes his eyes were glowing red. That's the only story I heard. In fact, I thought this was a very isolated incident."

These two stories seem to be part of the evolution of the contemporary legend, and they provide two key elements that would define the stories that were to follow: a mill-related death and glowing red eyes. The story would continue to evolve, and the "vat of lead" from the 1950s was replaced by the late 1980s with concrete. It was also by the late 1980s that tales began to circulate about the spirit known specifically as "Red Eyes."

"Red Eyes—I am watching you" graffitti, 2016. Photo by Dale Jarvis.

"Eyes are seen in the tower," one woman told me, "red eyes that are said to be from a man who died while building the mill." A second woman told me that people used to hang out at the mill and "would see a worker's daughter who died there in one of the towers."

"I heard that, apparently, it was a man killed during construction," a third woman told me. "He fell into a cement mixer or something like that, and I think he was built into the place. At night people would say 'Be careful of Red Eyes!' It was just an eerie place to be around, even in the daytime. I was only up there once at night, and not for long."

A Glovertown man who heard the story in the 1990s told me much the same thing: "He was a worker that fell in the pour when they poured the concrete for the tower. They never got him out. He got stuck in the walls, and he is still there." Yet another man told me the spirit was one of the construction workers who was blown off the top of the building while the mill was being built. "You can see his red eyes glow from the top once a year on the date it happened," he added. "Some people say he was pushed." Others blame an explosion for the man's death.

The abandoned mill, Glovertown, 2016. Photo by Dale Jarvis.

I posted a request for information on social media and was almost immediately contacted by someone on Facebook who wished to remain anonymous.

"I'm born and raised in Glovertown and spent my teenage years in 'the plant,' as we like to call it," he told me. "I've heard of the story, and I'll tell you what I know if you want some info."

I wanted some info. So I called him up to get his version of the Glovertown urban legend, which he too had learned in the 1990s:

"Most of my teenage years were spent at the plant, the old sawmill. There is a swimming hole next to it, and as teenagers, that is where we went. It is only a couple minutes off one of the roads, so it was just tucked away enough that your parents couldn't see you drinking. The story has been passed down from the older kids to the younger kids, to scare the crap out of them. When I was a kid, the story was that when the mill was built by a Norwegian company, industrial safety was non-existent. One of the construction workers did not show up at the end of his shift, and they found his body where it had fallen down inside one of the towers. He died there, and they say that to this day his red eyes haunt the plant. If you were there by yourself, you would see these travelling red eyes following you around."

While the Red Eyes story seems to have started in the late 1980s, it continues today; like most legends, it grows and changes in the retelling. By 1997–1998, a new variant had emerged, possibly based on one of the 1980s versions involving a worker's daughter. In November of 2016, a twenty-four-year-old resident of Angle Brook Road shared with me that version of the story:

"During the construction of the old mill, one of the workers lived close by the construction site since he was from out of town. He remained in Glovertown on the weekends, and on one of his days off he took his young daughter to the Terra Nova River to go swimming. The man wasn't a swimmer, so he would watch his daughter from a safe distance, reminding her to not go out too far due to the fast current. He took his eyes off his daughter for a split second, and when he looked back she was out farther than normal and couldn't swim back in. He jumped in to save her, but not being a swimmer himself, he was unable to reach her, and she ended up being taken away by the current. She was never found. The father was grief-stricken, and not knowing how to cope with it, he climbed to the top of the mill. Some people say he hung himself in the tower, and others say he jumped. According to the legend, there were reports of glowing red eyes at the top of the tower and in the tunnel that locals call 'the two doors.' Some say that on a quiet night you can still hear his little girl crying out for help, and sounds of him sobbing."

To make the corpus of Red Eyes stories just a bit more complicated, there is a sub-genre of local tales where the spirit is called either "Cement Block Sam" or "Cement Box Sam."

"His name was Cement Block Sam, and he was working on the mill," Paula Feltham told me. "This was talked about mostly in the late 1980s and early 1990s. It was our generation who came up with him!

"He fell and landed in cement and died. They continued to build the old mill, but Sam's ghost was stuck in the cement. On a good night, his eyes would glow red in the cement. We always looked for him, and spent many days and nights hanging out in the mill, but could never find him. It was a huge deal during our teenage years. Though we always looked for him and talked about him, thank goodness we never saw him!"

Whether you call him Red Eyes or Cement Block Sam, I am one hundred per cent certain that Glovertown's glow-in-the-dark ghost did not actually originate in Glovertown. There are many stories worldwide about people killed on construction sites or buried alive in concrete, with their ghosts demanding attention ever after. I have written before about an almost identical legend which is told about the Main Dam at Junction Brook, part of the system that feeds into the Deer Lake hydroelectric station. The firm of W. I. Bishop poured a total of 26,000 cubic metres of concrete to construct the dam, and a man (also named Sam!) was apparently buried alive in the slurry. The Deer Lake version of the glowing "red eyes" is the ghostly light from poor Sam's hard hat, illuminating his final resting place.

The similarities do not stop in Deer Lake. The Manila Film Centre in the Philippines is said to contain workers within its concrete foundation, with their ghosts haunting the facility. A large concrete bridge at the edge of Sidney, Ohio; the concrete pilings of the US 190 Mississippi River Bridge; and the Norris Dam in Tennessee: they all have almost exactly the same story. The most famous of these "buried in concrete" legends relates to the massive Hoover Dam on the Colorado River, a legend which has been debunked time and time again but which still floats around as a "true" story.

So, old Red Eyes is certainly an urban legend and one that from anecdotal evidence was not told in Glovertown much before the early 1990s. People who grew up in the town in the 1970s, for example, do not seem to be familiar with the legend.

But the abandoned mill site is not the only potentially haunted location in Glovertown.

"My mother sometimes used to say she thought the place was cursed."

Those are the words of "Molly," who grew up in the community, and the "cursed" place was her family home. It was a small one-level building on Riverside Road. The house had been constructed by Molly's grandfather and great-grandfather circa 1978. It was yellow with brown trim and had been built for Molly's mother and father.

For the period between 1980 and the 1990s, a series of strange happenings took place in the dwelling. The house had three bedrooms, but the weirdness was focused on the smallest bedroom in the house.

"I think my mother thought it was strange, but she never really believed in those types of things," says Molly. "She always brushed it off, maybe so we wouldn't be frightened. When my oldest sister was around four, she slept in the smallest bedroom, and once she got older it became my room."

When Molly was about fifteen years old, she left her guitar leaning up against her bedroom wall while she was doing homework. All of a sudden, the guitar strummed by itself.

"I wasn't long running out of there," Molly says.

As a young girl, she had a recurring dream of a white gloved hand emerging through the wall near the closet. The hand would wave toward her as if beckoning the child to come closer. Unbeknownst to Molly, her sister had experienced the same vision in the room when she was the same age. Neither sister told the other at the time, and it was not until the girls were much older that they shared the story and found they had both dreamed of the same ghostly gloved hand, urging them nearer.

"Neither of us knew we shared the same dream until much later in life," says Molly, "which I thought was really bizarre!

"This probably has nothing to do with it, but our house was constantly being hit by lightning," adds Molly. "Broken

VCRs, broken TVs, the telephone was hit once, and the light switch for the bathroom, all on different occasions."

Perhaps all that spare electrical energy had something to do with another strange happening in the house.

"My sister and I were alone listening to a Rod Stewart tape in her bedroom," Molly relates. "When we were finished, she got in the shower, while I went in the living room to watch TV. When all of a sudden, on comes the Rod Stewart tape. I thought, 'Okay, I just forgot to turn it off.' So I went in the bedroom and turned off the tape. I went back in the living room. A few minutes later, the same thing, on comes Rod Stewart again."

Molly knocked on the bathroom door and told her sister something weird was going on, but the sister didn't believe her.

"So I went and turned off the music again," she continues. "We went back in the living room, and guess what happened? Rod Stewart again! This time my sister came out of the bathroom, and we were both pretty horrified."

"I can't remember what happened after that, but I can never hear Rod Stewart again without getting the creeps."

If you are visiting Glovertown, you can take your pick as to which supernatural entity you want to spend your time with: Red Eyes, or Rod Stewart. I might opt for Red Eyes, personally.

THE WEBBER

Western Newfoundland

One of the most intriguing contemporary legends I have come across from Newfoundland is the story of The Webber—a terrifying, woods-dwelling creature with webbed hands, who loves to catch and devour children, campers, and canoodling teenagers. I first heard the story from actor and writer Dave Sullivan in 2009. Sullivan's version concerned a disfigured child born with a white face and webbed hands. The parents kept the child chained up, hidden away in a basement, so disgusted were they by what they had produced. The creature eventually escaped, a man was disembowelled on a country road, and a legend was born.

Once I started to investigate the story further, I was intrigued. It is a story that is known in the area between Stephenville and Deer Lake but largely unheard of on the east coast of Newfoundland. The Webber seems to be primarily a west coast legend, and several of its older origin stories place it around the Harmon Air Force Base in Stephenville, which operated between 1941 and 1966.

The legend has migrated north and east, with versions found along the Great Northern Peninsula and Labrador, and with one outlying variant told about the Heart's Content Barrens area between Carbonear and Heart's Content. The stories incorporate tropes found in other contemporary and urban legends like "The Hook Man" and "The Boyfriend's Death," but there are always similarities between many of The Webber's origin stories—he is born with webbed hands (and sometimes feet) and then is either abandoned, lost in an accident, or murders his unfortunate parents. It then goes on to live in the wild and to terrorize, maim, and/or eat innocent passersby.

The Webber made a special guest appearance on the Halloween 2016 edition of the *Sunday Night Geek* podcast. *Sunday Night Geek* is a Corner Brook–based Internet radio show about pop culture, fandom, and people's geeky interests. The show is hosted by Jeff Keeping, Angela Street, and Sean Michelin. The trio were largely unaware of the legend, but folklorist John Bodner of Memorial University's Grenfell Campus stopped by the podcast to share some tales, including a fantastic archival version of the creature's origin story. Bodner's version featured an ambulance accident, a shocking amount of blood and death, and the creature clawing its way out of its mother's womb. It's worth a listen!

Some stories about The Webber are short anecdotes, with very little in the way of narrative. Carolyn, who heard the story in the 1980s on Change Islands, via a fellow from Lewisporte, remembered the webbed hands and feet, and not much else, other than he "crawled out of the bogs and could swim anywhere, so we were not safe even out on Change Islands."

Other stories, however, are very detailed.

These longer stories about The Webber break down into

two rough sections, with an origin story or backstory, and then a contemporary legend about The Webber's current activities. While the origin stories are similar, there are differences depending on the place and time the storyteller learned the story. Below are several different origin stories, presented chronologically and indicating the story's point of origin.

Debbie Robbins, Carmanville, summer of 1978:

The Webber was a man-like creature covered in hair who migrated between Nova Scotia and Newfoundland every seven years. The creature had webbed hands and feet which enabled it to swim to and from Newfoundland.

Nadine, Stephenville, circa 1987–88:

A couple was having a baby and the lady went into labour. The couple were trying to find the quickest way from the Hansen highway to the hospital and took "Igloo Road," which was a long dirt road that brought you quickly from Cold Brook to right next to "base" near the hospital. On the way, the ambulance broke down and the woman was forced to give birth right then and there on Igloo Road. The baby was born and had webbed hands and feet and had fangs and immediately bit off its own umbilical cord and scurried off into the woods, and was never seen again, until . . .

Eanie Clarke, Blaketown, circa 1990:

Many years ago, a man and woman in their fifties found out they were going to be first-time parents. They were very

> *excited as they thought at this point in time a child was not to be. The months passed quickly and, at last, he was born. Unlike most newborns, he was grotesquely deformed. He had webbed hands and feet and some other physical deformities: an unusually large head, for one, and long claw-like fingernails. News quickly spread, and he was nicknamed The Webber Baby after his oddly webbed hands and feet. The parents vowed to love him and protect their child. They decided to raise him at home and keep him inside at all times so no one could make fun of him. People forgot about The Webber Baby. As he grew he was unusually strong and hard for them to handle. In his teens he was too hard to control, so the parents moved him into the basement and brought food down to him. As the couple reached their seventies, they decided they could no longer care for him and protect him. They decided to bring him to Carbonear to a home that took people who needed care. They put him in the car and headed away from the only home he had ever known. Later that night, their car was found flipped over in the woods several feet from the road. The elderly couple were torn up and dead. When they were first found they were thought to be cut by all the glass, until they looked inside the car to see the material on the roof slashed apart by what looked to be a wild animal. Their son was nowhere to be found. He had escaped into the woods. He made sure he would never be locked up again by anyone. On occasions when you think you see someone up ahead on the road on the Barrens, only to have them vanish when you get there, it's just The Webber Baby.*

Jenelle Duval, Brownie camp outside Corner Brook, possibly Pasadena, 1992:

The Webber was born deformed, with webbed hands and webbed feet, and lived in isolation near Pasadena with his unwed mother who was embarrassed by his appearance. He was feral, lived outside, and when his mother passed on he still lived. He was said to feed on the children who attended the camp that was built on his mother's land. It scared the piss out of us when we were kids. They said if you went by the water and wandered away from the camp, The Webber would get you.

Anastacia Hopkins, Camp Ashanti, Black Duck Siding, 1994:

An American couple were living on the base in Stephenville during WWII. They had a baby boy, and to their horror, he was born with webbing between his fingers and toes. They decided to fly back to the States to have the webbing removed, but their plane crashed just outside of town and the parents were killed. The baby survived and grew up to hunt children who were out wandering around the woods after nightfall. Depending on who is telling the story, the plane went down in the Fox Island River area or where there used to be a campsite mainly used for the Beavers and Boy Scouts, Camp Ashanti, in Black Duck Siding.

Matthew Howse, Silver Birches Cub Camp, near Pasadena, Spring 1994:

A family was involved in a car accident along the highway near Pasadena. It happened at night, and the car went far enough into the woods that no one noticed it for a few days.

The kid survived the crash, but a bunch of birds attacked him and injured his hands as he defended himself. He couldn't find the highway and went into the woods and raised himself up in there. His injured hands healed into duck-like webs, and he ate whatever he could find. He was particularly fond of young campers.

Kristin, Deer Lake, circa 1998–2002:

A boy and his family were driving to Corner Brook when they got into an accident near one of the off-ramps near Pasadena. Their car crashed and caught on fire; the parents died on impact, but the boy survived. However, he struggled to get out of the car, and the skin on his hands melted and burned while trying to escape. Once he escaped from the car, he didn't know where he was and got lost deeper and deeper into the woods. Once his hands had healed, they were webbed. He has been living in the woods ever since and would prey on campers that ventured out alone.

Erin Boyd, Camp Ashanti, Black Duck Siding, 2002–2004:

A young couple from Stephenville were happy and excited to be expecting their first child. Early ultrasounds revealed that the baby had webbed hands and feet but was otherwise in good health. In the seventh month of pregnancy, the mother started to experience sharp pains and was rushed to Corner Brook late at night. But the ambulance never arrived. The next day the ambulance was found to have crashed off the highway just outside Black Duck Siding. A horrifying sight met the police officers' eyes: the three paramedics were found clawed to death, and the mother-to-be was found with a gaping hole in her abdomen. The baby was nowhere to be found. For months police investigated the accident and tried to find a rational explanation. As time went on, they were eventually forced to close the case and come to a terrifying conclusion: the baby had somehow clawed its way out of its mother's belly and attacked the paramedics, causing the accident.

The Webber, as the child came to be known, is rumoured to wander the woods around Black Duck Siding, attacking hunters, fishermen, and any lost souls who entered the woods. His favourite meal? The young campers who frequent Camp Ashanti with groups of Girl Guides, Scouts, cadets, and school trips. To this very day, he can often be heard circling the cabins at night, waiting for a brave child to venture out into the darkness, alone.

Other than living in the woods, lurking in ponds, and preying on helpless campers, what does The Webber do with his spare time?

Here, we move into the second half of The Webber's narrative, and most of the legends I collected follow a pattern well-known to people who study contemporary legends. One good example comes from Ryan, who heard about the creature on the Northern Peninsula circa 1991. His best friend had returned from a trip to visit family in Labrador, and when he got back, he told four or five of his friends a cousin's story. Ryan remembers,

". . . a family had been camping in a gravel pit down a woods road, and when they went to leave, the car wouldn't start. The mother and child stayed in the car while the father went to get help. It was very foggy and misty, and they fell asleep in the car. They were woken up suddenly when someone pounded on the window, but when they looked, there was just a webbed hand covered in blood. It went away, and after a while, a police officer showed up and helped the mother and child but told the woman not to look back. When she did she saw pieces of her husband strung up in the trees and the word 'WEBBER' written in blood across the hood of the car."

Nadine from Stephenville heard a similar story circa 1987–88. In her version, The Webber lived in a shack along what was known as Igloo Road. She says,

"Igloo Road had many 'make out' spots. A young couple decided to head in up there for some alone time. After a few hours of romance they decided to leave, but the car would not start. The guy decided to go get a friend who lived nearby to get a boost, but the girl had to stay with the car. She fell asleep. Not long after she awoke to a 'tap tap tap' on the roof. It scared her so much she passed out but was awoken to police cars and an ambulance. The officer said, 'Come with us, please, but do not look back.' As she was led to the police car, her curiosity got the better of her, so as she entered the back seat she glanced back to see her boyfriend hanging upside down, dead from a tree, blood dripping from his mouth landing on the car going 'tap tap tap.' It was said that The Webber got him!"

Debbie Robbins has one of the earliest versions of the tale, which she heard in Carmanville in the summer of 1978:

"The last time it was in on the island, fourteen years earlier, it was suspected to be involved in a brutal murder of a young man. He and his girlfriend were driving along the road toward Gander when they ran out of gas. The man knew there was a station up ahead a couple or three miles so said he'd walk there, get some gas, and walk back. He told her that while he was gone she should lock the car doors and keep them locked. A two-mile walk there and back took a long time, and after a while the lightly falling rain made her sleepy and she drifted off. While she dozed she thought she could hear a steady tapping on the roof of the car; thinking the rain was coming down heavier, she ignored it and continued to doze. Much later she woke to the flashing of red and blue lights and an RCMP officer tapping on her window. She rolled down the window, and he told her to exit the car slowly and follow him and to be sure she didn't look back. He asked her three times to promise him she would absolutely not look back. The woman did as she was told until she reached the cruiser. About to get in the car, her curiosity took hold and she finally looked back toward the car. There on the top was the mangled body of her boyfriend staring at her with large dead eyes. The tapping, she was told later, was indeed the rain, but it was striking a nerve on one of his torn fingers, causing it to tap . . . tap . . . tap . . ."

This story, which has appeared in a variety of modern pop culture retellings, is based on a contemporary legend which writer Jan Brunvand calls "The Boyfriend's Death." In his book *The Vanishing Hitchhiker*, Brunvand states that the earliest version of the story was collected in 1964 by folklorist Daniel R. Barnes from an eighteen-year-old at the University of Kansas, though it is related to older legends such as "The Hook" and "The Roommate's Death." The legend follows the same pattern as The Webber story: a parked couple, an abandoned girl, the mysterious scratching or dripping sound, and the daylight rescue. There is generally a warning (such as "don't look back") and then a breaking of that warning (she does look back, and sees her husband/boyfriend dead).

Memorial University professor of folklore Paul Smith included a British version of the tale in his 1983 collection entitled *The Book of Nasty Legends*. Smith's story, called "Out of Petrol," follows the exact same pattern, with the boy leaving the girl alone while he gets gas. She locks the door, falls asleep, and is awakened by a steady thump, thump, thump on the car roof. She is eventually rescued by police, who tell her not to look back. She, of course, does look back, and sees an escaped mental patient "bouncing her boyfriend's decapitated head up and down on the roof."

Brunvand notes that the telling of "The Boyfriend's Death" often takes place "in spooky situations, late at night, near a cemetery, out camping, or . . . occasionally near the site of the supposed murder." Brunvand goes on to write:

> On a literal level a story like "The Boyfriend's Death" simply warns young people to avoid situations in which they may be endangered, but at a more symbolic level the story reveals society's broader fears of people, especially women and the young, being alone and among strangers in the darkened world outside the security of their own home or car.

The Webber story as told in Newfoundland is clearly a campfire story, told specifically in those spooky situations to frighten kids at overnight camps. Tellings of the story seem, with a couple exceptions, to concentrate around camps for children on the west coast of the island. Several storytellers remember learning about the creature at Camp Ashanti, currently run by the Newfoundland and Labrador Council of Scouts Canada. The camp's website notes that the camp has a large waterfront, tenting sites, a cookhouse, and cabins which sleep thirty-six in bunks.

"The camp has streetlights," adds the website, encouragingly, so as long as you stick to the lit paths you should be fine.

Other campers cited West Haven Camp near Pasadena as the point of origin. Angela Noseworthy learned the story in the mid-1990s at West Haven and told me she "always imagined The Webber as a child abandoned in the forest, swimming or crawling around in shallow streams." One camper told me, "I think eventually the story got banned because kids were scared, but in the early to mid '90s this one was a big part of camp at West Haven." Kristin learned the story at the same camp and told me the campsite "had a saying that the first person to arrive and the last person to leave were always prime targets for The Webber. Everywhere on the bunks and in the cabins were creepy carvings, such things as 'The Webber was here' and 'I saw The Webber and lived.'"

The stories continue to this day, with the gleeful help of a modern generation of camp counsellors. Alan Taylor is one example. He currently runs the West Haven Camp in Pasadena.

"I have been going to camp since 1988 as a young seven-year-old and have grown up with The Webber story," he told me. "We have even had counsellors outside the bunkhouse at night scratching at the windows, and underneath the bunkhouse scratching on the floor." His version of the legend ties the monster's origins inextricably to West Haven:

"The Webber was an eight-year-old boy who came to West Haven Junior Camp one year. He was born with webbed feet and hands and had trouble making friends. His parents thought camp would be a good idea, as they had both gone to camp as children and had made some great friends. Unfortunately, he did not fit into camp and was teased about being different, so much so that one day during a camp favourite game, 'Survival,' he was last seen running down an old beaver trail. Once the game was over, he did not return, and a search party was sent out but could not find him. Eventually, the search was called off and the boy was thought to have drowned in Deer Lake or to have been taken by an animal. Since then, there have been many sightings of a boy with webbed hands and feet covered in mud running down the trail and off into the woods. The trail is now known as 'The Webber Trail.'"

So there you have it, an internationally known contemporary legend, grafted onto a Newfoundland origin story, and told deliberately to scare kids at camp, complete with named geographic locations to aid in the transmission of the legend.

It is an entirely fictional story and nothing more.

That is what you would like to believe, at least.

While I was researching the history of the Webber legend and its multiple versions and variants, I got an intriguing note from Kharis Samms. She told me of something astonishing that had happened to her parents in Tilt Cove in 1973, the year before they got married, and five years earlier than the earliest version of the legend I had collected. She learned the story from her father, a man who, she says, is "as honest as they come." He told her of his experience with deep conviction and was certain of what he had seen.

"Mom and he were out for a drive and decided to park on the wharf in Tilt Cove," she told me. "It was dark and the car was left running, with the headlights shining out across the water. Then up over the edge of the wharf in front of them came a man-like creature with webbed feet and hands that stood up in front of the car on two legs. It used a ladder to climb up over the breakwater barrier at the end of Tilt Cove wharf. Its head had fins that came out of the sides of its face, and it was a blackish-green colour.

"My parents weren't long getting out of there," she adds. "I'd get no embellishments or tall tales from Mom. When I mentioned it, she matter-of-factly described the creature just as my dad had, like something from the 'Black Lagoon,' she said, and followed it up with the admission that she'd never told anyone because they would think she was crazy, something my mom most certainly is not."

Samms went on to tell me that, three days later, there were reports of a similar sighting in a nearby spot called Indian Burying Place, now a resettled community. In the Indian Burying Place encounter, the creature climbed up out of the water into a punt that was moored in the harbour and then slid back out again, vanishing beneath the waves.

"I am sure my parents saw something that night," she finished. "Perhaps it was your Webber!"

CHAPTER FOUR
Locations of Mystery

One evening in late fall, my boyfriend and I went for a drive up Signal Hill. It had been a nice fall evening, with a clear sky, and a brisk cool wind in the air. While we were parked by Cabot Tower looking down over the city, a shroud of fog crept in and quickly consumed the top of the hill.

When we realized how thick the fog had become, and that we could not even see the city or Cabot Tower, we decided it would be best to drive back down the hill. As we were driving around the first big turn going down the hill, I exclaimed "Watch out!" and my boyfriend slammed on the brakes.

There, in front of our car, facing toward us in the middle of the road, was a man barely visible through the fog. He was wearing a long, dark grey coat and a salt and pepper–style cap. Then, no sooner had we looked toward each other, the man turned to face the side of the road, took a few steps, and vanished before our eyes before reaching the other side.

Instantly we both froze and felt a cold shiver run down our backs. After a short moment we began to drive again in silence. Once we were close to the bottom of the hill, we broke our silence and asked each other in unison if the other had seen what happened.

To this day, whenever we see the fog roll, in we talk about the spectre with the salt and pepper hat we saw that foggy evening on Signal Hill.

— Adapted from a story told by Maggie Courish, November 2016

Packing Minted Money. Illustration by Louis Rhead, circa 1915.

BURIED TREASURE AND GHOSTLY GUARDIANS

Clarke's Beach, Bay Roberts, Port de Grave, Torbay, Musgrave Harbour, Bonavista, Shoal Bay, and Money Point

From where I sit writing this in Clarke's Beach, Conception Bay, I can look out my front window and see the two ranges of hills that frame the harbour. To the south is Long Harry, which divides Clarke's Beach and South River from Cupids. To the north I can see Vinegar Hill, with Otterbury and Bareneed beyond.

I love that I live in a spot where stories and place are so interwoven.

A man from Bay Roberts once told me a story about Vinegar Hill. His grandmother had lived in Clarke's Beach, and when he would visit as a child, she would tell him ghost stories, including one about the hill. Local legend maintained that a pirate treasure had been buried on Vinegar Hill and that the ghosts of buccaneers lingered on the spot, forever guarding their unclaimed booty.

Lisa Wilson has done some oral history work in that part of Conception Bay and has recorded two additional buried treasure legends from that region. The first is from Olive Strickland, who told Wilson about a man who moved to the Bay Roberts area and discovered a buried treasure.

"He was down there, I've heard Dad telling, in this little shack he had built, you know, down toward Mad Rock, wasn't it?" Strickland says, "Down Juggler's Cove."

The man found something of value near Mad Rock and decided he needed to get out of town with it rather quickly. He bought a roll of sail canvas and was later seen with something wrapped up tight in the canvas, fastened with rope.

Vinegar Hill in the fog, overlooking Clarke's Beach, May 2017.
Photo by Dale Jarvis.

"They said it took him and two more men all they could do to get that up on the dray. And he carried it up and he got aboard the train. No one ever heard tell of him after. He went on."

Locals whispered he had found money, but no one ever saw exactly what he had wrapped up in all that canvas.

"It had to be something. It was all they could do to lift it aboard," says Strickland.

The second legend that Wilson recorded was from Greta Hussey, of Port de Grave, who remembered stories of a buried treasure on Green Point.

"Oh, ever since we were born it had been talked of," says Hussey. "It was talked about another one in Ship Cove Pond, in a barrel, but after a while the barrel was gone, you know. See, it was close comfort for the pirates. This is where they used to run from the ones that was after them. Oh, I've got all of that stories. But the one about the money, they came from Quebec one time and a guy tried to . . . but they didn't go in the right place. See, their instructions was to walk so many steps in a certain direction and turn in another direction, and there was a big rock there with an arrow into it, but they tell me that the arrow is pretty faded now, but they knew where it was, I suppose."

According to Hussey, the Green Point treasure was taken up, found by someone much like the Mad Rock treasure.

"The person who told me," says Hussey, "and he's dead and gone, he said, 'I acquired one piece of the money.' But I tell you, there'd have been more than one. We walked over it time and time again and didn't know it was there. We knew it was somewhere, or we thought we did."

Buried treasure stories, like the one at Vinegar Hill, often come with attendant ghosts. There is certainly no shortage of them in Newfoundland and Labrador. There are rumoured treasures buried on Signal Hill in St. John's, on Tracey Hill in Red Bay, and at Gallows Cove in Torbay. Each of those has a ghostly guardian of one sort or another, ranging from a headless African pirate to a ghostly dog. Writer L. E. F.

English noted in the *Newfoundland Quarterly* in 1956 that "at Motion Head near Torbay there is yet another chest, and the ghost in this case is a woman who glides through the air and emits unearthly cries. . . . At Cann Island off Musgrave Harbour, a treasure rests secure; impenetrable darkness shrouds the unlucky seeker who essays to delve on the rocky isle for the elusive chest."

Two men attempted to dig up a pirate treasure on Green Island, Bay of Islands. One of the pirate crew has been sacrificed to guard the loot, and when the men started digging, it did not take long before the ghostly guardian got to work. Researcher Lara Maynard uncovered the story as told by one of the men's grandsons, Horace Davis, and printed it in 1995:

> . . . After digging down about four feet, they struck what appeared to be a big iron box. At that very second there came a roar, like a roar of wind, that blowed sand all around them in a whirlwind, completely filling in the hole they had digged, and when they looked behind them they saw that the sod had been blown off the ground about the same shape and size of a coffin with a hole about the same depth as the hole they had digged. There wasn't a ripple on the water and the weather was calm again. They received such a fright that they both started to run, and Freeman Taylor stumbled and broke his leg. John Davis bandaged it up with lobster lats and twine.

The Bonavista Peninsula hides another treasure with a ghostly protector, which was reported in the *Journal of American Folklore* in 1895:

> At Bonavista, somewhere down the Cape Shore, there is an immense treasure, hidden long years ago by pirates. These pirates, after concealing their booty, sailed away in search of further plunder, leaving one of their number to guard the spot, first binding him by a solemn oath to remain till they returned. Years passed away, the unfortunate watchman shuffled off this mortal coil, and nothing but his spirit was left to watch the place. His friends have doubtless long ago departed this life also, and the ghost is so tired of his job that he makes this splendid offer: If anyone will go alone at midnight and shed blood at the spot (any animal will do to kill), that ceremony releases him from his obligation, and the person performing the kindly office can have the treasure. One of the most intelligent men in Bonavista told me that the story was told him by a man to whom the late pirate had volunteered the information. No one has yet been brave enough to venture.

Not to be outdone, Shoal Bay, located south of Petty Harbour, has six pirate ghosts guarding a valuable treasure. I found a reference to the tale in a fabulously titled publication called *The Town Crier's Grab-Bag of Newfoundland Folklore*, published circa 1976.

> Many claim that there are seven mounds of earth each side by side there. Six of these are graves of men who volunteered to stay ashore and watch over the seventh mound which is said to contain the treasure. People have walked overland to this spot, but no one

> has ever stayed all night. To go there by boat means scaling the cliffs, and for some reason, each time this is tried, loose rocks fall from above. These are supposed to be thrown by the ghosts of the six pirates.

The richly named Money Point also has an issue with shifting stones. Money Point is located about a mile from the now-abandoned community of Ireland's Eye, at the southwest end of Trinity Bay. There, a large pile of rocks is said to hide a fabulous treasure. The rocks are said to look like they were put there by hand. In a recorded interview done in the late 1960s, an Ireland's Eye man remembered both the pile of rocks and a strange story associated with it.

"They had to be put there, carried there," said the man. "There is no place around where the rocks are piled up, like they are at Money Point. I've heard them say that a person was digging for it one time, and when they went back in the morning, the rocks would be placed back again. They'd go up and move them one day, and when they'd go up the next day the rocks would be back."

There are Money Point legends up and down the Atlantic seaboard. There is a Money Point in County Cork, Ireland, and another Money Point in Chesapeake, Virginia, on the southern branch of the Elizabeth River. The Virginian Money Point was named, as local folklore goes, for treasure the pirate Blackbeard buried off of the shores of Money Point.

Yet another Money Point is located near Ingonish, Nova Scotia. It was named after a cove where a French galleon was purportedly wrecked. For years after, gold coins kept washing ashore, giving rise to a local legend spread by old-timers.

They said that one could stick a piece of tar on the bottom of a long stick and pluck up gold and silver coins close to the shoreline.

Legends move and blend together, so I am curious about the Trinity Bay Money Point story. Is it possible that the early settlers in Ireland's Eye, moving in from Conception Bay and from Dorset, England, brought stories of ghostly pirates and buried gold with them? Or is there truly something hidden under that strange pile of stones?

One Trinity Bay story tells of a man named Paddy who heard about the Money Point treasure and travelled to Ireland's Eye with a metal detector. Apparently, he left empty-handed, and no money was ever found. So, if the treasure remains hidden at Money Point, or at Shoal Bay, you might still have the opportunity to strike it rich.

Just be on the lookout for ghosts and for falling rocks.

FATHER DUFFY'S WELL

Salmonier Line

Several years ago, whilst travelling in Scotland, I stopped along the bonny shores of Loch Oich and found myself at the Well of the Seven Heads.

According to legend, the land once belonged to two brothers who were murdered by seven relatives. A cousin of the two brothers sought revenge, got an army together, tracked down the unlucky seven, and chopped off their heads. The seven heads were washed in the well at Loch Oich before being presented to the clan chief of Glengarry as proof of retribution.

Traditional watering places have often been imbued with layers of legendary meaning, and many public and private wells are treated by locals as special, almost sacred spaces. "Wells are mysterious things to most of us," writes folklorist Philip Hiscock, "and as with other locations of mystery in human life, folklore has grown up about them."

While holy wells are fairly common in Europe, we have very few here in Newfoundland, though two stand out. One is a hillside Mi'kmaq well in Bay du Nord devoted to St. Anne, and the other is Father Duffy's Well, on Salmonier Line. Father Duffy's Well comes with a miraculous origin story, curative powers, and possibly even the ability to grant wishes.

Reverend James Duffy was born in Ireland around 1797 and came to Newfoundland in 1833 with a group of priests who had volunteered to assist Bishop Fleming. Duffy eventually became the first parish priest of St. Mary's, a position he held for sixteen years.

His time in St. Mary's was eventful, as he became embroiled in a conflict with a local merchant about the site of a new church. The merchant had a fishing flake constructed to block the entrance to the church, and Duffy gave orders to the parishioners to tear it down. They did so, and the merchant (who was also the magistrate) had Duffy arrested and charged with leading a riot.

Over the next year, the priest had to travel back and forth several times between St. Mary's and St. John's to deal with court cases, trips which he made on foot. Along the way, he rested at a spot in the woods between Riverhead and Holyrood. It was at this spot in the woods that things got interesting, and there are several versions of what transpired.

My favourite version is found in the research conducted by Barbara Rieti and included in her Ph.D. thesis on file at Memorial University. In her thesis, she relates a short story told to her by one of her informants:

"In the car on the way to Mr. Joe's house, he told me the legend of Father Duffy's well," she writes, "where Father Duffy struggled with an evil spirit and overcame it when he struck the ground and water welled out."

In a 1926 article in the *Newfoundland Quarterly*, Rev. T. J. Gough of Portugal Cove described Duffy as "tall, broad of shoulder and well fitted to cope with hardship." In my imagination, I can see a pugilistic, broad-shouldered priest combating fiercely with an evil figure both horned and caped, Duffy picking up the spirit and dashing him to the ground like a professional wrestler, holy water bubbling up at the point of impact.

Father Duffy's Well circa 1948, Salmonier Line. Photo courtesy Memorial University of Newfoundland—Digital Archives Initiative.

I suspect, however, the truth of the legend was much less athletic or theatrical. It is more likely that the good Father Duffy chose that spot to camp because there was already a spring there. As Gough writes,

"We can . . . easily imagine Father Duffy and his guide halting halfway their journey, in that lonely spot, to take a scanty lunch and to drink from the pearly crystal Spring Well. Perchance, too, in his many travels across the Chisel Hill Country from Fermeuse or Cape Broyle to Salmonier, he made this his camping ground for the night. However, that may be, popular tradition says: 'Father Duffy blessed this Well, and our forefathers, wishing, no doubt, to see some resemblance in Fr. Duffy's Well and the Holy Wells of Ireland, invested this simple mountain Well and its surroundings with a sacramental character.'"

That "sacramental character" included a belief that the water from the well had healing or medicinal properties, and the well became a regular stopping place. People began to perceive it as a holy place, and its fame spread.

By April 1880, two decades after the death of Father Duffy, the well was so well-known that it was referenced in the *Evening Telegram* in a slightly scandalous joke about one of Newfoundland's governors. A gentleman travelling between St. Mary's and Holyrood saw a painted signboard on the path. When he asked his cabman what it meant, the man said,

"Once upon a time, there was a well underneath that mark. It was called 'Father Duffy's Well;' and many a weary traveller quenched his thirst with a draught of its coolin' water. One day the Governor happened to travel this road, and he stopped short where that mark is and took a drink. The well has been dry ever since!"

I am uncertain if the comment is meant to refer to the governor's ability to drink or to imply that he was so unholy he undid the priest's good work of creating the well in the first place.

The governor was not the only politician to visit. In 1925, a group of distinguished gentlemen of politics and business arrived in Corner Brook as part of a Canadian tour, a tour which previous to their arrival in Newfoundland had included visits to Montreal, Toronto, and Niagara. After celebrations in Corner Brook, they set off for Grand Falls, and then Placentia. But before they continued on to St. John's, the "Imperial Parliamentary Delegates" made one last stop, at Father Duffy's Well.

"Here," declared the *Evening Telegram*, "Hon. W. J. Higgins briefly recounted the story attached to the spot and explained the mystic powers of the spring by which the wishes of all who drank of its waters were fulfilled."

In December of 1934, the *Newfoundland Quarterly* included an ode to Father Duffy's Well, attributed to one "P.K.D."—a figure I suspect to be journalist, editor, educator, Justice of the Peace, Commissioner of Affidavits, and amateur folklorist Patrick Kevin Devine. The poet writes:

When lured by dreams of salmon streams
And sylvian beauties rare,
The tackle stowed you take the road
That leads to Salmonier,
Observe the sacred duties
Which all travellers compel
Drink from the cool and limpid pool
Of Father Duffy's well.

Tradition tells of early days
How Father Duffy found
A semblance of water
Just oozing from the ground.
He scraped away the turf and clay,
As thirst did him impel,
And very soon, we had the boon
Of Father Duffy's well.

In gratitude to God he knelt
And blessed as holy ground
That it may be a sacred spot
Through all the ages down.
When bridle path to highroad turned
And axemen came to fell,
Inviolate be kept the state
Of Father Duffy's well.

An elixir for man and beast
Provided for all time,
Secluded from life's arid road
In shade of fir and pine,
Refreshing weary travellers
Inspiring them to tell
How oft exhausted men were saved
By Father Duffy's well.

Then devotees who learned its worth
Adorned and cleared the place,
Safeguarding perpetuity
For all the human race.
They swept unsightly objects from
The precincts of the dell
And made a "Fort of Paradise"
Of Father Duffy's well.

Cursed be the man that dare profane
This loved and sacred shrine,
And make excuse "material use"

So callous is our time.
Commercial use may dollar bring,
But never can excel
The sentimental heritage
Of Father Duffy's well.

The spring at that time fed into a small rectangular rock pool. In 1935, the Knights of Columbus replaced the pool with a grotto, which has been added to and still stands today. Eventually, the spot was made into a provincial park (it saw 5,000 visitors in 1963), and today it is a picnic and rest spot. One visitor reminisced of a road trip along the Salmonier Line in 1987:

"The truly bright spot was Father Duffy's Well, where weary travellers could pull off the road and drink the freshest, coldest water imaginable. Oh, how in a child's mind it seemed to take forever to get there. Flat tires ruled the day—inner tubes had to be removed from tires, patched with a dubious combination of rubber patches and cement—a lengthy procedure. Today's modern paved road bears little resemblance to that of yesteryear, and Father Duffy's well is upon you before you've hardly started."

And so, I had to make my own trip to Father Duffy's Well. I came back from my pilgrimage with a bottle of (somewhat murky) water from the spring, which sits in a tall glass jar in my office. I have no desire to test out its potency just yet, but I am saving it for such a time when I either need all my wishes fulfilled or feel the desire to experience the legendary benefits of that "elixir for man and beast."

FOGO ISLAND'S MANY SPIRITS

Fogo Island

Fogo Island, off Newfoundland's northeast coast, has always had a strong storytelling tradition. Stories were often told in the winter, in the fishing sheds where gear and nets were mended, and where punts were repaired and built. At times, storytelling took on an almost competitive quality, with one man telling a tale and the next man trying to outdo him. This tradition was described by fisherman Isaac Primmer of Fogo Island in this way:

"There was a certain way to tell a story, you know. Some had a knack for tellin' stories, jokes, one thing and the other. They'd make a good story out of nothing. . . . One would try to outdo the other, you know. . . . Skipper Chris might tell a story about a man counted to be a good shot. Well, that would start it off, every man, then, have to tell a story that he heard. Some, you know, would add a bit here and there to make the story good. A good storyteller knew how to tell a story, keep everybody interested."

In November of 1989, folklorists Gerald Pocius and Mark Ferguson interviewed Barr'd Islands fisherman and former mayor Bill Godwin about his life and work with the fishery. In their chat, Godwin spoke about the role of storytelling on Fogo Island:

"There'd be a lot of stories told, years ago, old-time stories. And you believed them stories! There'd be a lot of ghost stories, and things they seen when they were boys, you know. And they'd have you make believe this. Growing up, we'd be scared to come home at night in the dark, no lights, all we had was a lamp on the wall, an old lamp. And Mother would turn that right down if I was out, turn it right down low, you'd just see the flicker of it till I came in, and then I'd blow that out before I went to bed. . . . My uncles and my dad would be putting us on, so it would be interesting to us to pass away the time. Half them stories would be all probably made up or some damn thing. . . . They'd make up stories, and get us a little scared, and wondering."

This tradition of Fogo Island ghost stories is well documented, and in 1999, the Fogo Island Literacy Association added to that documentation with the publication of a small book called *Tales of Fogo Island*, compiled and edited by Della Coish. The publication was designed as an easy-to-read book about local life and culture, for use with adult learners in literacy programs. The book contains short stories about losses and rescues at sea, historical tales, tragedies, remedies and cures, and a few ghost stories, including two Fogo Island stories about headless ghosts.

The first headless phantom was spotted by a man named Lynch, of Island Harbour. Lynch was on his way from Payne's Harbour to Butt's Point when he met a man on the road dressed in a black suit of clothes. When Lynch spoke to the stranger, he got no reply.

"This made him curious," writes Coish, "so he tried to

get a better look. Mr. Lynch almost jumped out of his skin when he realized that the figure in front of him did not have hands and did not have a head."

Before Lynch could shout out for help, the man in black vanished. He ran to his house and told his family. Once he convinced them of what he had seen, the family decided to call in the priest.

"As it happened, the priest was in Island Harbour that evening and arrived at the Lynch home in minutes," says Coish. "He asked Mr. Lynch to tell his story and describe where it had happened. Then the priest convinced a few people to go with him to the place where Mr. Lynch had seen the figure."

Upon reaching the spot of the haunting, the priest offered up a few prayers, and then all returned home. According to local folklore, the priest refused to ever speak of the event again.

The story of Mr. Lynch's vanishing headless spirit is mirrored by another tale from a neighbouring community. A woman from Fogo was walking home when she became aware of a man walking in front of her. Thinking it was her brother, Val, she called out to him.

"The man stopped for a moment but then began to walk faster," says Coish. "The lady picked up her pace to catch him, but the man also sped up. She soon became annoyed and shouted, 'Don't run away from me, Val, I knows who you is! Stop right now and wait fer me!'"

"Val" refused to stop, even though she called out several times. She hurried to catch up, and as she did, she noticed that the figure she had believed to be her brother was missing his head.

She caught up with the headless figure and, bravely, reached out to touch him. As soon as she did, the apparition vanished. Now properly frightened, she ran the rest of the way home. The following day, the family received sad news: a close relative had been killed fighting overseas.

A different ghost story from Fogo Island concerns a spot named Banks (or possibly Banks's) Meadow. Fogo native Barry Penton informs me that Banks was a Fogo name in the 1800s. According to the Anglican Church Diocesan Records, William Banks, a bachelor of Fogo, married spinster Jane Waterman at St. Andrew's Church in Fogo on the fourteenth of April, 1844.

"The last record I have is of a John Banks in 1883, who was a planter in Back Cove," says Penton.

Near Back Cove, there is also a Banks Cove. And given the family was in that area, it is likely the meadow was named after a member of the Banks clan.

"It's the field down below Brimstone Head," says Penton. "Locals refer to it as Second Field."

The Banks Meadow story was recounted to broadcaster Hiram Silk by a woman named Julia Wells. According to Wells, one evening in the early part of the twentieth century, a girl and her aunt were going to a meeting. Flashlight in hand, they followed the path up through Banks Meadow.

When they got partway across the meadow, they saw a man. He wore a little short coat like men wore at that time. As it was a cold night, he had the collar turned up.

"There's a man there," said the girl, pointing him out to the aunt.

"Yes," she said.

When they drew near him, the girl spoke to the man.

"Good night, sir," she called out, but he did not answer. The girl made to step one way, and he stepped back. The women passed by, and the girl looked behind them. The man was still there, standing still. She looked back again, and he was still there.

When the girl looked back a third time, the man had vanished from the middle of the meadow.

"Aunt Liz, that man is gone!" she cried.

"Oh no!" said the aunt.

"Oh yes he is, he's gone," said the girl. At that point, the two women made their way through the meadow as fast as they could.

At that time, many people in the cove claimed to have seen the man in the meadow. It was said that he was more like a shadow than a man. Even those who got close to him could not recognize his features.

One night in winter, the same girl was heading home, alone. The snow lay crisp and undinted. As the girl came up to the meadow, there was not a footprint to be seen in the snow.

She could see the lights in the houses of the cove and could hear dogs barking, but for some strange reason, she couldn't find the path to get home.

No matter which way she turned, she couldn't seem to find the path across the meadow. She turned around and went back to the place she had started from. Then she set out a second time, with the same result. When she got to the meadow, there was not a footprint anywhere, and no matter what she tried, she couldn't find the path.

The girl went back down to her cousin's house instead.

"You've got to go home with me tonight," she told the cousin. "I can't get home!"

The cousin walked her back up to the meadow, and when they got there, they found that the snow was all trampled to pieces, just to one side of the path.

When the girl looked, she saw a set of a man's footprints alongside her own.

"It don't look like I'm the only one out tonight," said the girl. "There's someone gone astray there."

The Town of Fogo, June 11, 2016.
Photo courtesy Paul Asman and Jill Lenoble, Flickr (CC BY 2.0).

The cousin got the girl home safely, and she put the incident out of her mind. A week later, however, she was visiting the home of the only woman in the cove to have a radio. A group had gathered to listen to the radio and were telling stories.

The group started talking about a man who got lost coming up across the meadow the week before. He had crossed it many times, but nothing strange had ever happened before.

The girl asked when he had gotten lost and discovered he had tried to cross it just before she had.

"He wasn't the only one," she told the crowd, and then shared her strange tale.

"There was something there," she said. "I couldn't get home."

The girl's father told her that there had been a grave there on the meadow at one point but that nothing remained to mark it.

The communities of Fogo Island have a strong link to their past, and the future of the island seems tied to its traditions, its culture, and its stories. While the location of that grave in the field might be forgotten by most, the spirits of the past have a way of lingering on and making their presence known. If you are one of the many who now venture to Fogo Island to experience its charms, take a moment to look back over your shoulder. You never know who you might see standing in the middle of that meadow.

THOSE BLOODY ROCKS

TILTING, ALEXANDER BAY, NEW PERLICAN, HANT'S HARBOUR, AND RED INDIAN LAKE

It was a good day for gardening, and for murder.

Michael Turpin and Patrick Murray were setting potatoes in their garden at Sandy Cove, Tilting, Fogo Island, on June 13, 1809. As they worked away, they were attacked by a group of Beothuk. Although he did not know it, Michael Turpin was about to become a part of both history and local geography for generations to follow.

"The two men got such a fright that they ran in separate directions," writes Della Coish. "Patrick Murray ran toward Tilting. The Indians followed close behind. They almost caught him when he got stuck in some mud near Reardon's Rock. Luckily, he was running so fast that his shoes came off, and he continued running in his bare feet."

A woman named Foley caught sight of Murray running with the Beothuk running behind him. The woman had a spade with her, and she raised it up and pointed it at the pursuers.

"They must have thought it was a gun, because they turned and ran away," writes Coish. "Murray continued running until he fell at his wife's feet with two arrows in his back. They removed the arrows, and Murray survived."

Michael Turpin, in the meantime, was in serious trouble.

"He tried to escape by swimming to a schooner anchored in Sandy Cove. However, the Indians easily captured him and dragged him back to shore. There, they pushed him onto a large rock and chopped off his head. Michael Turpin's blood ran over the rock and seeped into every crack and pore in its surface. The blood remained on the rock for many years, and it soon became known as Turpin's Rock."

Dramatic stuff indeed, though other writers have presented the story with alternate details, such as a 1900 mention in a book by Devine and O'Mara which has Turpin scalped instead of beheaded. This version is repeated in later retellings, including a 1987 article in the *Decks Awash* magazine.

These stories may have some origin in a historical event, and I was told by one man that he was the descendant of the woman who pointed her spade at the Beothuks. But there are other parts of the story that nudge it into the category of contemporary legend, particularly the bit about the bloodstained rocks, with gore in "every crack and pore."

The idea of a bloodstain which cannot be washed away is a recurring motif in legend and myth. What student of Shakespeare can forget Lady Macbeth's struggle to get out, out, that damned spot of blood? In the Lady's case, it is not just the visible reminder of the blood of which she cannot rid herself: "Here's the smell of the blood still," cries the Lady in dismay, "all the perfumes of Arabia will not sweeten this little hand. Oh! Oh! Oh!" The motif is so well-known that folklorists even have a number and name for it: "E422.1.11.5.1. Ineradicable bloodstain after bloody tragedy." The bloody image wells up time and again, not just in literature, but also in the folk tradition, and, in Newfoundland, local place names.

St. John's teacher and artist Bruce Brenton told me, "There was a place in the Alexander Bay area called 'Bloody Bay Reach.' Supposedly there had been a massacre having to do with Europeans and Beothuk. Not sure who massacred whom . . ."

New Perlican has "Bloody Point"—a spot with its own story of violence related to the Beothuk people. As Dwayne Tuck told me, "Local history has it that that is near an area where aboriginals were drove onto a point of land and killed." Grant Tucker wrote to tell me that "Bloody Point, New Perlican, probably gets its name from the reddish colour of the rocks (iron oxide), less romantic, perhaps, but more likely. A local tradition has suggested that there was a battle between the French and English or Europeans and Indians." Some have put the blame for the blood-soaked rocks on the French naval leader Pierre Le Moyne d'Iberville, who attacked New Perlican on February 9, 1697, though there is no historical evidence of any great massacre.

James P. Howley notes in his book *The Beothuks or Red Indians* that "(a)nother tradition was current to the effect that on one occasion 400 Indians were surprised and driven out on a point of land near Hant's Harbour, known as Bloody Point, and all were destroyed."

There is little evidence outside of Howley for such an extermination. There are also doubts that there were even 400 Beothuk available in the area during that time period to drive into the sea. But people in Hant's Harbour still believe that the massacre happened on a point of land in their community. One woman from the area told me, "I am not sure if that is called Bloody Point, but I do know that there were about 400 Beothuks driven in the water from a point in Hant's Harbour, according to the history of Hant's Harbour." Grant Tucker concurs:

"As a boy growing up in Hant's Harbour, I often heard that the place where the Beothuks were driven into the sea was near where the lighthouse is today; it was never called Bloody Point but Custer's Head. Local folklore recounts that one Indian was surprised by fishermen rowing along the shore; he went ashore and, with his canoe 'on his back,' scrambled up a gulch and disappeared in the woods."

Howley goes on to document a couple more bloody locations: another Bloody Point, at Red Indian Lake, where two marines were killed and beheaded in 1811 by the Beothuk; he also quotes the Rev. W. Wilson, who notes, "A place called 'Bloody Bay' on the north side of Bonavista Bay has often been named to the writer as a place where frequent encounters had occurred with the Red Indians." There is yet another Bloody Point on or near Sound Island, Placentia Bay, and a Bloody Pond in the interior of the Avalon Peninsula, in the northernmost half of the Avalon Wilderness Preserve.

Historical fact, oral history, and local legend often get mangled together to the point where it is difficult to differentiate one from the other. Most folklorists would agree that the stories we chose to tell say more about us, the tellers, than they do about historical truth. Newfoundlanders seem to love stories about Beothuk massacres. In an informal conversation with one local archaeologist, he stated quite firmly that most of these stories of battles and mass killings have no basis in historical fact. Ingeborg Marshall, the best-known expert on the history and ethnography of the Beothuk, is also clear on the subject. She writes,

"Two recent histories of Glovertown (in the district of Alexander Bay) also claim that Englishmen, rather than Beothuk, were killed there. According to Harold Stroud, people in the area believe that the name Bloody Bay is based on the late-eighteenth-century killing by Beothuk of a family of Kearleys, or Carleys. Watson Lane was told that Bloody Bay may have received its name on account of the murder of eleven fishermen by Beothuk; a twelfth man who hid under his overturned boat survived. This is said to have occurred at Curley's Cove, a small cove on the north side of Bloody Bay. These stories suggest that the names Bloody Bay and Bloody Point have spawned a number of conflicting traditions, all concerning bloody encounters; yet there is no actual proof that any of these tales—including that related to Howley in the 1880s—were based on facts."

And since there is no way that I can argue with Dr. Marshall's knowledge on the subject, perhaps it is on that note that we shall end this whole bloody business.

THE BOULEVARD'S BLACK AND WHITE GHOST

St. John's

Two ghosts, separated by a gulf of fifty years? Or one ghost, who slumbered for half a century before returning to haunt the living? Come with me for a late-night stroll down the Boulevard, and you can judge for yourself.

The Boulevard is located along the northwest edge of Quidi Vidi Lake in St. John's, running between King's Bridge Road and East White Hills Road. The Boulevard was created in the early twentieth century, following the gift of land to the city by a gentleman named Mr. Robert Cole, of King's Bridge. Cole's obituary, printed in the St. John's *Daily Star* on the eleventh of December, 1918, noted the following:

"A man of patriotic temperament, he took an active interest in civic and political life, and any movement for the betterment of the city or its people had in him a warm advocate, a fact which he demonstrated some years ago when he offered a considerable portion of his property to create a boulevard at the western end of Quidi Vidi Lake."

The Boulevard forms the southern boundary of the Mount Carmel Cemetery, at the western end of the street.

The cemetery was consecrated by Bishop John Thomas Mullock on July 3, 1859, who wrote in his diary on that day: "Today I consecrated the cemetery at Quidi Vidi. Thousands were present. The weather awfully hot. Temperature 84 degrees in the shade."

As warm as it might have been on that day in 1859, there are a few things about the Boulevard that might give you the shivers, today. Several years ago, a gentleman named Harry contacted me to share a story of a strange experience which he and a group of friends had shared one November in the early 1960s. Harry wrote:

"Kids used to trout, so one night down at Quidi Vidi between Field's old house and the bandstand I caught a four-pound brown trout (graveyard worms were the best). My friends playing spotlight near Conway's old stone house heard about my prize, and all rallied with poles to the head of the pond. Six of us lined off along the shore on a misty November night, with our spotlight fighting over a few worms. When Tommy looked up, he saw this man slowly walking toward us. We spoke to him, but he did not answer, so we shone the light in his face, and the beam seemed to go right through him. He was scruffy and dressed in turn-of-the-century clothes: a light-coloured jacket with light-coloured pants, laced-up boots, and an old hat pulled down over his forehead. He did not speak but kept intentionally walking toward us. Tommy shouted out to us that he was wearing a mask. At that point we all looked at this ghostly figure and dropped our poles and ran. When we looked back he had vanished."

The six friends gave a statement to the Criminal Investigation Division of the Newfoundland Constabulary, and the police were on scene approximately fifteen minutes later.

They recovered the boys' fishing poles and flashlight in a search of the lakehead. The police also conducted a search on Circular Road and Empire Avenue that did not turn up any pedestrians that night.

"We know he did not get past us on the dimly lighted boulevard," added Harry. "If we were ever to see him again we were to phone the police, they said."

But nothing happened. The scruffy figure in his old-fashioned clothes and hat had vanished from the Boulevard, never to be seen again.

Or had he?

Fifty years later, "Karen" had a strange experience while driving alongside Quidi Vidi Lake, shortly after midnight on Remembrance Day in 2011. Karen was in St. John's, from out of town, and had just dropped off a friend when a strange apparition came up onto the road in front of her car.

"I was driving along the Boulevard by Quidi Vidi Lake, between the bandstand and military base," Karen remembers. As she did, something caught her eye, moving very quickly up the bank from the direction of the pond.

"I saw a smoke-coloured figure come over the bank and onto the road directly in front of my car," she describes.

Thinking she was about to hit a person, the woman reacted immediately.

"I slammed on the brakes," she describes. " I'm glad there was nobody behind me, because I would have gotten rear-ended."

When she did, the figure in front of her simply dissolved into the midnight air.

"I did not just see that!"

"It happened all in a matter of split seconds," Karen says.

"It was very, very fast. It was just like somebody walked right out in front of my car. I'd never seen anything like that before in my life. I couldn't believe it had happened. I was on my way over to my sister's house, and I told them as soon as I got there."

While she had experienced strange things in the past, meeting the figure on the Boulevard was Karen's first time seeing a full-bodied apparition. She was shocked by how detailed the figure was.

"It was a man about 5'9 and slim build, dressed in older-style clothing, wearing a salt and pepper cap, linen shirt with the sleeves rolled up, suspenders, and linen trousers. His clothing appeared to be messed up, or worn in. I could see that he had dark hair and stubble, and he looked to be in his thirties."

Karen describes the man as being a dirty, smoky colour, almost more like he was an antique photograph than a real person. Her description is remarkably similar to the haunting reported in the 1960s.

"He looked like he was in a black-and-white picture, and when he dissipated, it was just like cigarette smoke!

"I will never forget it," she says.

So we are back where we started, with a question. Is that stretch of the Boulevard home to one ghost, or two? If that particular monochromatic haunting only occurs once every fifty years, you might need to wait till 2061 to find out.

In the meantime, a location closer to the historic Mount Carmel Cemetery may also be haunted. Consider what happened to Cindy Pearson and her friend Rhonda Whalen in the fall of 2012:

"She was in the passenger seat and I was the driver. As we

were driving past the graveyard heading west toward King's Bridge Road, she yelled at me to watch out. I didn't see anything. I asked her what the heck was she yelling about. She replied by saying, 'Didn't you see the guy who just hopped the graveyard fence and ran across the road?' I asked what he looked like, and she described him as being in his mid-twenties with blond hair in a mullet-style haircut, wearing tight jeans and a jean jacket."

Pearson had seen nothing pass by the front of her car; her friend was convinced she had seen a ghost in denim, straight out of the 1980s. It might be easy to dismiss it as a singular event, but others in that spot have also witnessed a ghost taxi pulling out of the graveyard late at night.

From the ghost of the '80s, to phantom taxi cabs, to our mysterious black and white ghost, there is clearly something spooky happening along the Boulevard.

CHAPTER FIVE
Darkness and the Light

The settlers had many superstitions and were obsessed by a belief in the presence of ghosts. It was common to hear of a man, who, while rowing across the harbour, had seen a phantom French ship, with many soldiers aboard, also crossing. Others had seen an Indian ghost following them from one settlement to another.

Their superstitions were legion, and I shall mention only one. During the seal hunt, if a successful hunter saw anybody throwing blood out of his boat into the boat of another, a fight was sure to follow, because the hunter believed that his luck was being stolen.

— J. Morgan, "Recollections of Harbour Deep," 1957

"Smarra." Illustration by Tony Johannot, 1846.

THE DEVIL AT THE DANCE

Brigus and Spaniard's Bay

I was in Bay Roberts having a chat with Mike Flynn, a local historian and author. We were talking about the Newfoundland of yesteryear, and Flynn was a wealth of knowledge, sharing some great bits of local folklore, including legends about ghosts and buried treasure.

"There's a flat rock by the side of the road near Beaver Pond in Brigus, and there is a footprint in it called the Devil's Footprint," he told me.

"Were there stories about people meeting the Devil?" I asked.

"As a matter of fact, now that you've jogged my memory, my mother was telling me one time they were at a dance in Spaniard's Bay. There was a girl at the dance who apparently wasn't all that attractive to males.

"'I'd dance with the Devil himself, tonight, if he was here,' said the girl.

"A few minutes later, this guy came along and asked her for a dance," says Flynn. "And when they were out dancing, waltzing, she looked down, and he had hooves rather than feet.

"These are scary stories, you know, for a kid!" Flynn added.

Scary, but fabulous. For a folklorist and storyteller, when I hear a story like that, it is like a prospector striking gold. It is another great example of a contemporary legend, or what some people might call an urban legend, though they are not always told in an urban context. And while they might be contemporary in their telling, the stories sometimes go back a long, long way.

"Pas de Deux." Illustration by Arthur Rackham, 1907.

The Devil at the dance story is one of these stories. I have heard and read various versions over the years, some set in Newfoundland, and many others from other places. Some of those stories go back centuries.

One of my storytelling friends is Gail de Vos, who teaches at the School of Library and Information Studies at the University of Alberta. She is also a great storyteller, whose specialty is telling contemporary legends. In her book, *Tales, Rumors and Gossip,* de Vos includes a European version of the legend that dates back to 1875. In her version, a servant woman went dancing at a ballroom on one of the last Sundays before Lent.

"Around midnight, she saw a handsomely dressed stranger with black hair and eyes that glistened like onyx, coming toward her to ask her for a dance," writes de Vos. "She took his arm with pleasure as they began to dance with perfect grace, but faster and faster."

One of the musicians noticed that the dashing stranger, like the one in Spaniard's Bay, had cloven hooves. He changed the tune from a waltz into a hymn. The dancer whirled the girl across the ballroom and right through a window.

"The girl was found lying on the green grass in the garden covered with broken glass," writes de Vos. "The Devil had disappeared."

He is a tricky character, Old Nick. So, if you are out for a time in Spaniard's Bay, or enjoying a walk through the picturesque streets of historic Brigus, and you happen to meet a handsomely dressed stranger, just remember this tip from the stories of old:

Check out his feet before you agree to a dance.

READING THE CARDS

Joe Batt's Arm

Every so often, I get emails or letters from people with stories about strange happenings or odd bits of Newfoundland and Labrador folklore. It is one of my favourite perks of doing what I do. Sometimes, like with the note I received from Francis Furlong, they grab me immediately.

"Hi," wrote Furlong, "have you ever heard stories about playing cards coming to life?"

Could a folklorist or storyteller wish for a better opening line in a letter?

Furlong told me that his mother has a lot of stories from Joe Batt's Arm, featuring ghosts of British redcoats, children's voices in the house, people walking around all hours of the night, a local monster with only eyes on its face, a man whose hair turned white after an encounter with the fairies, and the Virgin Mary in her blue dress helping children lost in the woods.

He told me that while his mother's memory is not as great as it once was, she has one story that stands out in her memory in particular. His mother's name is Leone Miller, maiden name Etheridge.

"She grew up on Etheridge's Point in Joe Batt's Arm and always told us stories from there," he explains.

"Mom tells a story about growing up in Joe Batt's Arm. She was walking to a friend's house, and she had her mom's playing cards, also the same cards that her mother would read like tarot cards. As she was walking, she dropped the cards and they scattered on the ground. All of a sudden, all the kings, queens, and jokers of all the suits came off the cards, like little people, and started dancing around her, then they fell back into the cards they came off of. She has told us this all our lives and swears to it to this day."

Joe Batt's Arm, June 10, 2016.
Photo courtesy Paul Asman and Jill Lenoble, Flickr (CC BY 2.0).

Playing cards in Newfoundland oral tradition often carry a whiff of something supernatural. I have heard stories about the Devil appearing at card games, and even of a family near Burgeo who vanished mysteriously, house and all, after playing cards on a Sunday.

But cards coming to life is a new story for me, and it reminds me tremendously of Lewis Carroll's book *Alice's Adventures in Wonderland*, which was always one of my favourite reads as a child.

The deck of cards in Furlong's story had something of a history in family lore. Furlong said that, according to family stories, these were the same cards his grandmother would put on her nightstand before she went to sleep.

"She would wake up later to find the cards spread out over her perfectly, like a blanket, each card end to end in perfect rows."

WICKED WITCHES

St. John's, Joe Batt's Arm, Comfort Cove, and Colliers

I have been collecting and sharing supernatural stories for a long time, and people know that I am always interested in hearing new stories. So, it is not unusual for people to approach me out of the blue, as they did with the previous story, with information they would normally not share with a complete stranger. The plumber who came to fix my bathtub had a story; the security guard at the airport had another.

One evening, a gentleman approached me and told me about a leaping witch in downtown St. John's.

The average person might not think that often about witchcraft in Newfoundland and Labrador. While ghost stories and fairy stories are more common or more popular in the telling today, there is a long history of witchcraft belief in the province. And while there are many good and sensible witches and new-age pagans in the world today, the term "witch" is still used to describe some aspects of the supernatural that are dark, strange, and mysterious, and which have nothing to do with the more modern incarnations of witchcraft.

Downtown St. John's, you would think, would hardly be a place where folk belief in spells and witchcraft would linger. But at least one dramatic story about an acrobatic witch and her actions survives from the area around Balsam Street, which runs between Queens Road and Livingstone Street.

The gentleman who told me the story said he heard it from his grandfather. The grandfather, as a boy, had lived in a row house across Balsam Street from a woman who was suspected of being a witch. The boy was up late one night, looking out his bedroom window on the top floor of the house. Peering across the street toward the house of the suspected witch, he saw the woman climbing along the outside of the building, close to the roofline.

Astonished, the boy watched as the woman clambered across the eaves. The woman, as if she knew she was being watched, suddenly turned to stare straight at the boy. The boy was petrified as their eyes locked across the dark downtown street.

Turning slightly, the woman tensed for a moment. Then with a great, superhuman spring, she jumped from her house, all the way across the street, and landed on the window ledge right in front of the terrified boy. She landed on the sill with such force that she cracked the window glass from one side to the other.

The boy fled. When he returned with his family, the woman was gone, but the crack in the window was still there. The window was not repaired, and the crack remained in the pane for years after as proof of the witch's feat.

A different jumping witch legend comes to us from the town of Joe Batt's Arm, on Fogo Island. Dean Penton learned the story decades ago from his great-uncle, who has since passed away.

"Legend has it that in the mid to late 1700s, residents of Joe Batt's Arm decided on a witch hunt, to banish all remaining witches from the community," writes Penton. "During the hunt, they came across the most powerful witch any man had ever seen. As they chased her to the edge of the sea on Etheridge's Point, she was cornered."

Sign marking the location of the witch's footprint, Joe Batt's Arm.
Photo courtesy Dean Penton, joebattsarm.ca.

In order to escape the angry mob, the witch leaped to an island in the middle of the harbour, leaving behind a molten hot footprint in the rock. From there she leaped once more to Brown's Point and was never seen again.

"Some say the witch drowned in her attempt to escape, others state she simply disappeared into the darkness and was never seen again," Penton adds. "However, numerous strange sightings and even screams of an unknown woman have been witnessed by many people over the centuries on Etheridge's Point."

Today, the impression of that witch's foot can be seen on a rock located at Etheridge's Point, and if you search carefully you can find the footprints left behind by her prodigious leaps.

The Etheridge's Point footprint is the most readily accessible, and if you are feeling brave, you can take off your footwear and try to match your bare foot to the print left in the stone. If it is a perfect fit, you might have some explaining to do, since the print features the mark of six longer-than-average toes.

Comfort Cove, near Lewisporte, is home to yet another witch legend, which came to my attention thanks to Kate Rideout. There, the witch is said to haunt a section of Comfort Cove Road. While her legend is not widely known in the region, a few local people know the story, and at least one man refused to drive the road alone because of it. Rideout and a few other people from Comfort Cove have seen the spirit first-hand.

The "witch" takes the form a strange green glow, slightly hidden behind a small hill along the stretch of highway. Local folklore maintains that once you see the witch's glowing form, a devilish presence will be your passenger in the back seat for the remainder of your ride home. The passenger is said to be either an unknown dark figure or the spirit of a dead person who had wished you harm when they were alive.

"I've seen a few ghosts before, and this one was the most worrisome I've seen," says Rideout. "She was just a green glowing light, and from the headlights I could see the parts of her that weren't glowing were black, like a dress. Once we passed her, my heart sank, and I was forced to look in the back seat. There was a man back there with a burnt-like face, just sitting looking straight ahead."

Once she got home, Rideout was reduced to tears and did not sleep that night, overcome as she was with the feeling of that strange man following her.

Rideout's father also had a run-in with the green witch of Comfort Cove Road, only a few hours before her encounter.

"He turned whiter than a sheet and just sped the rest of the way," she describes. "He didn't talk the rest of the night and just shakes his head when I bring it up."

Encounters with dark forces or strange figures led many Newfoundlanders in the historical period to come up with complex counter-charms and rituals to keep witches at bay. One type of counter-charm was the use of a witch bottle.

Molly (née Murphy) Quinn was raised in Philadelphia, but her family comes from Colliers and Conception Harbour, and she has spent her summers in Newfoundland since she was a girl. Quinn's grandmother, Alice McGrath Murphy, died in 2007 at the age of ninety-two. During those Newfoundland summers, Grandmother Murphy told Quinn more than a few tales.

"My childhood was filled with stories of fairies, 'Bloody Bones,' and more stories than I can remember," says Quinn. "My grandmother's mother was the midwife of the community. Many tragedies occurred in childbirth, and most were attributed to bad luck, the wrath of God, and some to a witch or bad person."

If you thought your bad luck was due to a witch's influence, you could make a witch bottle to break the curse.

"I know you were supposed to put things in them to remove curses," she says.

Generally, a witch bottle is made by filling a vessel with symbolic items like pins, darning needles, or fabric hearts, and in some cases, with urine. It was then corked. By trapping things in a bottle, the victim is meant to redirect suffering back on the witch responsible. Quinn's story involves a woman who had experimented with witch bottles, but who was unable to rid herself of whatever curse had attached itself to her and her family.

"Years ago, a young woman lost her husband rather tragically," Quinn relates. "She was always dressed in black and, having lost all faith in God, was said to have dabbled with witch bottles, believing her husband was taken from her wrongly."

Afterwards, the woman was never the same.

"She could always be seen near the large boulder in front of the cemetery, dressed in black and forever weeping for her lost love," describes Quinn. "One evening, a young married couple was driving across the cemetery hill in their sleigh. The woman was at the rock weeping.

"As the sleigh passed, she leapt in, touching the young groom with her hand," Quinn says. "Her icy touch immediately killed the young man. Because of her actions, she was cursed to mourn forever at the cemetery, always seeking her husband's return.

"I get shivers just thinking of it now," says Quinn, "especially because I visit that cemetery each summer to visit relatives' graves."

The use of witch bottles originated in Europe and was later introduced to North America. Ruby Andrews Moore, writing about superstitions in Georgia in 1892, notes that "to keep witches off the place, a black bottle containing iron nails was buried under the front doorstep."

One of my favourite witch bottle stories was recorded from around Chestertown, Maryland, and reported in the *Journal of American Folklore* in 1890. The witch bottles there were filled with what are known locally as "ground-puppies" or "ground-dogs."

"These names are given to some common species of salamander (Amblystoma). As many 'ground-dogs' as possible are to be put into a wide-mouthed bottle and buried under the threshold of the person whom it is desired to conjure, at the same time making crosses with the four fingers on the earth above the buried bottle. After a time the 'ground-puppies' will burst the containing bottle, and then they will find their way into the stomach of the person against whom the spell is directed, and kill him. They can be driven out by taking internally a tincture made by soaking May-apple root, or snake-root, in whiskey. It is safest, however, to consult a 'fortune-teller doctor,' if one has reason to suspect the presence of ground-dogs in his stomach."

Wise advice, I am certain.

Witch bottles in the Colliers area of Conception Bay may have a long history. Archaeological work in the nearby community of Cupids has uncovered remnants of Bellarmine bottles—a type of pottery jug with a distinctive human face design on the neck of the bottle. In the seventeenth century, they were sometimes employed as witch bottles.

An example of a sixteenth-century Bartmann (or Bellarmine) jug. Photo courtesy Museum August-Kestner in Hannover/Wikimedia.org.

A charred face from a seventeenth-century German-manufactured Bellarmine bottle was found broken on the cobblestones west of the dwelling house at Cupids. Archaeological work undertaken at Ferryland in 1997 also recovered fragments of Bellarmine jugs, and archaeologists Barry Gaulton and Catherine Hawkins reported in 2015 that roughly half of a large Rhenish stoneware Bellarmine bottle was found at Ferryland, and later pieced together in the lab. Bellarmine fragments were also uncovered from the Hefford Plantation, New Perlican.

Were these jugs used as witch bottles? We may never know, and certainly not all Bellarmine jugs were witch bottles. But some Newfoundland settlers knew of the tradition, and Bellarmine jugs seem to have been a favourite material for building counter-charms. In 1987, it was noted that of the 200 documented witch bottles found in England to that point, 130 were Bellarmine jugs. A similar bottle from the same time period as the Cupids jug was recovered from an archaeological site in the UK in 2004. Upon opening up the bottle, it was found to contain "bent pins, a nail-pierced heart made of leather, fingernail clippings, belly-button lint, and hair, all swimming in a bath of 300-year-old, nicotine-tinged urine."

It sounds like the perfect concoction to keep a witch (or anyone, for that matter) far, far away.

THE CAT WHO WASN'T THERE

St. John's and Carbonear

I got into a St. John's taxi cab, and the cab driver looked at me out of the corner of his eye.

"You're the ghost man," he said.

"I am the ghost man," I agreed, and waited, because when someone starts a conversation with me in that manner, they generally have a story. Sure enough, I was not disappointed. We talked for a little bit about where he had grown up on the Southside of St. John's, and I asked if he had ever heard stories about the fairies there.

"No, no fairies," he said. "But I do know that story about the kittens who came back from the dead."

This was a new one for me, and as we cruised down New Gower Street, I asked him to elaborate.

Apparently, a man on the Southside had a cat who had produced an unwanted litter of kittens. As was the custom in those days, the man put the kittens in a sack, took them down to the wharf, and tossed them into the St. John's harbour. He watched the sack fly through the air, land in the water with a splash, and then sink beneath the murky waters of the harbour. He waited as bubbles rose up from the depths, and then, satisfied with a job well-done, he headed home.

That night, the man heard a noise at his window. He looked up, in horror, I imagine, to see a line of ghostly kittens peering in back at him from the other side of the windowpane.

I have to admit that I was torn. As an absolute lover of cats, I was saddened by their drowning. As a lover of ghost stories (and as a believer in the old adage that you reap what you sow), I was delighted to hear that the evildoer was haunted by those revenant kittens.

For as long as humans have shared the earth with cats, we have known that there is something unearthly about them. From the ancient Egyptians to the modern day, there is always the whiff of something magical about our feline friends. In his book of light verse, *Old Possum's Book of Practical Cats*, the poet T. S. Eliot writes of the Original Conjuring Cat, Mr. Mistoffelees. In the book, the grandly named cat has the singular magical power to appear to be where he is not:

His manner is vague and aloof,
You would think there was nobody shyer—
But his voice has been heard on the roof
When he was curled up by the fire.

Amongst people who like to discuss the unexplained, this power is often referred to as "bilocation." Bilocation is the ability to be, or to appear to be, located in two distinct places at the same instant in time. Many of you who know cats, like our friend T. S. Eliot, might have had an experience with a Mr. Mistoffelees of your own.

For one cat-owning couple in the Georgestown area of St. John's, the phenomenon might go one step further: they may very well have a ghost cat. Both the husband and wife have had run-ins with the property's phantom feline. The house was built in the 1920s and was purchased by the couple in 1999. Since then, mysterious cat sightings have been a part of their daily life in the house.

"I've felt the cat brush against my leg," says the husband. "I've also had numerous occasions where I've come into a room and have seen a cat out of the corner of my eye, but then upon looking, the cat is gone."

The wife has had similar experiences.

"I would see a cat and think it was one of our cats," she describes. "I've seen the cat when I've been in the laundry room. I said to the cat 'it's not time for you to be fed yet' and when I walked out, all our cats were in the hallway outside the office. None of the cats had gone by me."

On another occasion, she saw the cat in the living room.

"It jumped off the rocking chair," she says. "There was no cat in the living room, and the rocking chair started to rock. That was creepy."

In 2006, the couple had a visitor from Ireland, a woman who claimed to have some psychic abilities. She told the couple about several different spirits she could sense in the house. After a while, the husband asked the visitor if she could sense any animal spirits in the home.

"Oh yes," the Irish woman said, matter-of-factly. "There is a ghost cat here, and his name is Septimus."

So there you have it, a phantom feline with a very distinguished name. Mr. Mistoffelees would be proud, I am sure.

In 1992, Daniel Penney, originally from Carbonear, came

home from school to find that his parents had gotten him a kitten.

"He was black with smoky-grey highlights going through his entire coat, so I decided I would call him Smokey," says Penney. "He became a pet unlike any we have ever had, and we bonded closely."

Smokey would usually sleep with Daniel in his bed.

"If he had been outside late and someone let him in the house while I was sleeping, he would push the door open in my room and hop on the bed," remembers Penney. "Usually when he did this, he wasn't quite ready to settle in. He would start by sitting by your chest, and if you didn't acknowledge his presence, he would start to purr so hard and loud you could see him rock back and forth. If I still ignored him, hoping he would let me sleep and go to sleep himself, then he would bawl ever so lightly, just enough for you to hear him."

If Penney did not give Smokey the attention he wanted, he would poke his owner's arm. Penney would have to pet the cat till it fell asleep, in order to get any sleep himself.

"He and I were inseparable," says Penney, "and if I went for a walk outside anywhere, he would tag along with me."

In 2007, the beloved cat grew feeble and sick. Much to the dismay of the family, there was little they could do, and the cat had to be put to sleep by the veterinarian.

"I brought him home from the vet and wrapped him in his favourite blankets, laid him in a wooden box my father had made for him, and we buried him in our backyard. After fifteen years we were all devastated, and our lives and home felt empty. I felt so guilty for putting him to sleep, even though I knew it was the right thing to do."

That evening, Penney fell into bed, exhausted. But he

could not get to sleep right away; the bed felt empty without Smokey. Eventually, he fell asleep.

"During the night at some point, I rolled over in bed, and for a split second, I opened my eyes," describes Penney. "Then I felt something hop up on the bed behind me. I heard the purring and decided to pet who I thought was my other cat, Rusty. But when I awoke and rolled over, it was Smokey looking right at me. When I reached out to pet him, he disappeared like he was never there."

Penney sat up in bed. He tried to figure out what had just happened.

"Though I was grieving, I felt at peace," he says. "As I was lying back down in bed to turn in, Rusty entered my room and hopped up on the bed and fell asleep. I've never seen Smokey ever again."

Penney acknowledges that some may say he just mixed up one cat for the other, though the two cats were of very different colours.

"I can't help but wonder if Smokey came back just to make my mind at peace, by letting me know he was okay and at peace himself, or if it was just lack of sleep with a mix of grief," muses Penney. "If it was just a mix of grief and lack of sleep, then the only thing I cannot explain is the weight I felt in my mattress, and the tugging of the sheets like I used to feel when he sat next to my chest!"

People have strong bonds with their animals, and I am certain that Penney is not the only person in the province with experiences with a deceased pet. I am glad that the visitation gave him some peace, and I would probably feel the same if I was in the same boat. The drowned kittens, however, can stay where they are over on the Southside Road.

HEAVENLY REPRESENTATIVES

Carbonear, Bonavista, and Heart's Content

In 2014, an elderly lady from Carbonear underwent open heart surgery. The night after surgery, she saw an ominous dark figure hovering in the corner of her hospital room. The figure was formless, appearing like a large black cloud. It terrified the woman, who whispered a prayer to keep it at bay. The next evening, a ball of white light appeared as if in answer to her prayers. The dark form disappeared, and her health improved dramatically. After a few weeks, she was well enough to go home. She is still doing well and living on her own in Carbonear. Though the orb of light has not been seen since, the woman is happy to know it is out there, somewhere.

"It put her at ease," the woman's personal care attendant told me. "She felt like she had an angel watching out for her."

Angelic figures or messengers from the other side often appear in end-of-life stories. Many people who have been around those close to death have either had strange experiences themselves, or have had those about to die confess to seeing otherworldly visitors, heralds, or guides.

Cindy Slaney-Miller experienced this when her mother, Betty, was in palliative care. One evening, while family were visiting, Betty informed them that there was another person in the room.

"She said her 'representative' was in the room," Slaney-Miller explains. "He was wearing a white suit. The next morning when I arrived, she asked me if I had thanked him for showing up last night because he really didn't have to be there, but she was glad he was, and again described what he looked like!"

The woman quizzed her mother about it, and she said that the man in the white suit was going to meet her later.

"It was a surreal thing," she says. "She totally convinced me that someone was there."

Nicole's story is similar. In 2003, her mother was in the late stages of terminal cancer. She was in hospice care, and her wakeful moments were less frequent. During those times she would frequently speak of, or wave to, a woman in the room with her at the hospital in Bonavista.

"We were never sure when she would slip away," says Nicole. "The only people she seemed to recognize were me and my dad."

On several occasions during her periods of alertness, Nicole would notice her looking off into a corner of the room.

"Occasionally she would smile or nod like she was answering a question or agreeing to something," Nicole says. "Finally, when it was her and I alone in the room, and after I had seen her smile and wave, always in the same direction, to her right, near the door to the room, I said, 'Mom, who are you waving at? There's no one there.'"

"I'm waving to the woman over there," her mother said.

She pointed, and Nicole looked, but there was no one there.

"I asked her again who she was waving at, and she told me that there was a nice woman in white who was standing in the corner," Nicole describes. "I tried asking her more questions but was never able to get straight answers while she was lucid. She did continue to wave, smile, and nod, and occasionally mumble something over the following days. She passed on March 1, 2003. It did bring me some amount of comfort to think that maybe there was someone there with her during her final days."

While the previous two stories featured a figure in white, not all heavenly representatives are so attired. Dee Payne's grandfather told her of a lady in a blue veil who appeared at the foot of his bed in St. John's on November 7, 1987.

"She took one look at my grandfather and shook her head," Payne says. "She walked to my grandmother's side of the bed and touched her on the head. The next day, my grandmother passed away due to a stroke.

"Grandfather often told us of the lady in the blue veil from that day, until he died himself eleven years later. It always struck the family as peculiar that the lady in the blue veil shook her head when she looked at my grandfather, and chose my grandmother, as my grandfather was always the one of poorly health, and my grandmother was as healthy as a horse."

Sometimes these visitors from beyond are the spirits of those who have gone on before. That is what happened to one Heart's Delight family during the last week of January 2000.

"The Sunday before my grandfather went to the hospital (we know now for the final time), he had a vision of my grandmother who passed just eight months before him. He looked a little downhearted when he came out of his room that morning, and seeing his expression, I asked what was troubling him. His response was, 'I seen her as clear as I ever did standing alongside of my dresser. When I put out my hand to touch her, she was gone.' I think she came to let him know they would soon be reunited."

BEDTIME WITH THE OLD HAG

Coming soon to a mattress near you

Dear readers, I have deliberately left this to be my last story with you, with the slightly devilish hope that it will be the last thing you read before tucking in for the night.

One of my best-loved Newfoundland and Labrador terrors is the Old Hag. Part ghost story, part dream, and part real experience, the Old Hag occurs where one is half-awake but paralyzed by seemingly ghostly forces. Some people feel the weight of someone sitting on their chest, others see a ghostly figure either above them or at the foot of the bed. Ofttimes she is described as an old woman, with long, tangled hair. If you have not yet met the Old Hag in person, count your blessings, for it can be a terrifying experience.

Lloyd Pike does not believe in ghosts, but his first encounter with the Old Hag was so vivid it made him wonder. In 1972–73, Pike was spending his first year as a teacher on Pass Island, on the southwest coast near Hermitage. At that point, Pass Island had a population of a few hundred people, with only two Jeeps on the island for transportation. Pike stayed at a boarding house in sight of the school at Mooring Cove. It was at the boarding house that Pike first met the Old

Hag, on an absolutely pitch-black night, so dark he could not see his hand in front of his face. Pike describes his experience in this way:

> There was a window next to the door, with an old-fashioned, handmade lace curtain on it. It was very dark, but you could see in the window a slight illumination, a little flick of light. That was the beacon light for mariners, which was up on the hill. That would constantly flick, and by that light, you could see the pattern of that lace curtain.
>
> I guess I fell asleep, but everything was so real I thought I was still awake. I was lying there, listening to the foghorn, waiting for sleep, and then I felt that someone had come to the door. Of course, I couldn't see anyone, because it was so dark, but I just knew someone was there. I waited for someone to speak, perhaps the landlady checking on me, or her mother, but nobody spoke.
>
> I waited, and then I had the sense that the person was walking into the room. The beacon was flickering in the window, the only bit of illumination you could see in the room. I was waiting for the shadow of someone to pass in front of that window, but nothing happened.
>
> Then I had the sense that the person was standing next to the bed, looking down on me. At this point, I started to get that little creepy feeling up the back my spine. This was odd behaviour. And then I had the sense that the person was moving through the bed. At this point, you would think you must know you

were asleep, but it wasn't like that. As they got to the point where I was lying in the bed and they moved through where my body was, I felt this bone-chilling cold. I had never felt so cold; I can feel it still, almost. It went right to the bone. I was lying there, getting more and more terrified all the time, and then the person moved through my body, and the cold went away and the warmth returned. It went to the wall, and then I felt the person come back through me again, and again as they passed through me I could feel that bone-chilling cold. All the while the foghorn was repeating its sound and the beacon was flickering.

Then, the second most terrifying thing: I knew the person was in the room, but I didn't know where. Then I felt hands reach up through the bed and grab me by the biceps and begin to pull me down through the bed. That is the moment I snapped awake, and I couldn't move. I'd never had an experience like that before. I absolutely could not move my eyes, and I swear I could still feel the pressure of the fingers on my biceps, pulling me down through the bed. I was very tense. I laid there a long, long time like that, and eventually movement came back to me, and the sensation went away from my arms, but the terror didn't. I was absolutely terrified.

Of course, the next day, when I told people, they said, "Oh, that was the Old Hag," and I said, "What's that, I've never heard of that?"

Pike's dramatic experience with the Old Hag is typical of many encounters: the sensation of not being alone, a mixing of dream and waking states, the inability to move or call out, and the feeling of being held down. The sensation of paralysis, sometimes combined with the sensation of being pressed down into the bed, is a common motif in Old Hag narratives.

In addition to the paralysis, it is common for people with Newfoundland hag experiences to see the creature herself. Julia was one such person:

"The Nightmare," by Henry Fuseli (1781), is thought to be one of the classic depictions of sleep paralysis. Image courtesy wikipedia.org.

"Before we moved back to Newfoundland, my family and I were staying at a bed and breakfast on Prince Edward Island. I woke in the middle of the night unable to move or call out. I was able to see the chair at the end of the bed, and sitting in the chair was a woman. She was dressed in clothes from the 1940s with the saddest face I have ever seen. Her eyes were black and sunken, and there was a feeling of despair that rolled off her. I closed my eyes, terrified, and woke in the morning."

Both Megan Somerton and her boyfriend have had run-ins with the Hag on Gower Street in St. John's:

"I've only experienced this once. However, I had heard about the Old Hag tale prior to this so knew exactly what was happening. I couldn't move, and I was screaming out, but there was no sound. My room was completely dark and I didn't see anything. I just closed my eyes and waited for it to stop since I knew I couldn't do anything. My boyfriend has a similar story, although more scary, in the same place. He said there was a very old woman figure all in black; all he could see was eyes next to him. It was pretty intense."

A sense of despair is often mentioned in such nighttime meetings. "Susan" grew up in St. John's and has been aware of the existence of the Old Hag legend since she was young. She believes she heard of the Old Hag first from her father, who had also experienced the nighttime terror. Susan herself has experienced the sleep-paralysis side of the phenomenon, but a few years ago, she woke up around two or three o'clock in the morning to encounter a different aspect of the Old Hag.

"It was sometime in the middle of the night," she remembers. "It was pitch black outside. Every so often, I find that I can't wake up out of a dream, and this is what happened. I tried to wake up, but I couldn't."

In her half-waking, half-sleeping state, the woman tried to scream but found she could not.

"I felt completely paralyzed," she says. "I guess that is the normal part of it, but what was different about this time was that I felt like I was being pressed on, like I was being stifled somehow. The particular thing about this time that was different was that I felt it on my face. It may sound weird, but it felt like hair or feathers, something ticklish brushing my face. I couldn't really identify what it was, but it scared the daylights out of me. I tried to scream, but couldn't scream. I couldn't move. Nothing.

"Finally, I came to and woke up, and I jumped out of bed," she says. "It was the biggest fright of my life."

When I interviewed Susan, she said there was a sense of sadness or darkness that seemed to accompany the Old Hag.

"I want to say it was malevolent, but I don't know if I'm being fanciful," she says. "But it was a bad feeling, like it was a witch or something with crazy hair or feathers. I don't know if it was a bird, or a woman, or something, but it was right up in my face. It was really scary. I've never heard anyone talk about hair or feathers before, but that was the definitive part of the dream."

While the Old Hag is most often associated with visions of creepy old women and the sensation of paralysis, it quite often includes noises, sounds, and other auditory elements. The phenomenon can take on many different forms, and so the feeling of hair or feathers brushing across one's face is, perhaps, not unusual. British researcher Dr. Paul Chambers writes, "In addition to sensing a presence in the room, many people report feelings of flying or floating, and anomalous noises and lights are also commonly reported."

The Old Hag can take many forms. While researching this book, a cashier at the Carbonear Foodland told me about getting the Old Hag, and how a white dog will appear at the end of her bed. A man from Corner Book told me how the Hag would appear as a dark, shadowy figure looking in at him from the doorway.

"The sheer terror and dread that I remember, seeing her in the doorway, was unbearable," he confessed to me. "It was like knowing that you were sharing space with something sinister."

Ashley Byrne was hagged in 2012 while living in Goose Cove on the Northern Peninsula, near St. Anthony. It was an experience she describes today as the worst feeling of her life:

"It was the most terrifying, unnerving thing that I have ever experienced! Horrible! I was lying on my side, facing my husband. The front of my body felt like it was on fire, and my back was colder than I have ever felt before or since. The room was so chaotic it was almost vibrating. I couldn't move anything except my eyes. At the foot of the bed was a long dresser. There were two children, little boys, sitting on the dresser looking at me. I could see a figure lying behind me, and then I felt ice-cold fingers run down my back. I can still picture the children I saw so vividly. The one boy was wearing a grey knitted sweater, and the other fellow was wearing a blue woollen salt-and-pepper kind of hat, and a white long-sleeve button-up shirt and suspenders. It is etched into my memory so clearly. All this happened in less than a minute. I was screaming my husband's name, or so I thought. The third time I screamed his name, everything stopped, was quiet and peaceful, and I could move."

Krista Wall experienced a similar creepy-children version of the Old Hag in Paradise. She saw them first around

2004, and then again about three years later, in the same house and same bedroom.

"I'm not sure if I would call it the Hag, or sleep paralysis. Twice it was the same dream: two children in the doorway of my bedroom, a boy and girl. I can still remember in great detail what they looked like. I can still picture the two I saw like it was yesterday. He had on a little jacket, grey with black buttons, with short-style pants and black boots. The girl had on a grey and white dress about knee length, with no frills, very plain, black boots with laces, and black tights. Her hair was down with a little curl at the ends. Both were blond. They just stood there in the doorway looking at me. I remember being cold. I tried to turn on a light—then realized I couldn't move, or scream. And I tried! Believe me! My grandmother also gets 'the Hag' fairly often. I remember being a young girl; Pop told me the demons had come for her. It frightened the daylights out of me!"

"I had the old Hag many times, but it comes in different ways," I was told by storyteller Tony Power of Branch. "It is as if you are paralyzed; it is like you're in a battle with evil, or falling off a cliff and waking up when you're only inches from hitting the rocks. Other times, this old woman appears at the foot of the bed and slowly crawls toward you, and tries choking the living daylights out of you before you wake. It is one of the worst experiences to have in your sleep."

Luckily, Power also has some advice for those who suffer from the Old Hag.

"If you make the sign of the cross on the roof of your mouth with your tongue, you will wake up," he tells me. "Holy water also helps."

In addition to holy water, keeping a copy of the Bible

under your pillow may work. Words, of one sort or another, have always been said to be an effective charm against the Hag. According to the *Dictionary of Newfoundland English*, one remedy for the Hag involves the afflicted party calling out his or her own name backwards. Eileen Balsom Matthews of Heritage New Perlican wrote me to say, "Hubby tells me years ago, in New Perlican, there was a guy who had it a lot, and his wife told him 'to say his name backwards three times really fast to get rid of it,' and apparently it worked!" Others have advised reciting the Lord's Prayer, either forwards, as one would normally, or backwards.

In 1896, the *Journal of American Folklore* printed the following "cure" for the Old Hag:

"A man at Change Islands, in the district of Notre Dame Bay, told me he had been ridden to death by an old hag, until a knowledgeable old man advised him to drive nails through a shingle and lash it to his breast when he went to bed, with the nails sticking up. With great solemnity he assured me that, thus fortified, he had just forgotten the world, when down came the Old Hag all aflop, but with a hideous scream she went 'off quicker'n she come on.' His rest has been peaceful ever since."

Some people are of the opinion that your sleeping posture has an effect on you being hagged.

"My father gets the Hag when he sleeps flat on his back," Sheila tells me. "He has for as long as I can remember. He doesn't have any visions but is always very tense and feels like if he relaxes, he will die; however, if he manages to move at all, even a pinky twitch, the Hag will break. In his mind, it is pretty much a life-or-death struggle. Sometimes he even gets mad at Mom since he is going through this and she doesn't help, but she is unaware of anything until it breaks, and either he wakes or mentions it in the mornings. He has had it happen multiple times in one night, and those nights he gives up trying to sleep in bed and goes downstairs to try to sleep in his recliner. I am pretty sure that is the reason he is donating his body to science once he passes—he doesn't want to spend eternity on his back!"

As for the Corner Brook man who was visited by the Hag every night from January until March? He moved into a different house.

"To the best of my recollection, I have not had a visit from the Hag since," he told me.

I have one last, final anecdote. It has been said, more than once, that simply reading about, talking about, or even just thinking about the Old Hag greatly increases your chances of getting a late-night visit from Newfoundland and Labrador's most terrifying nocturnal horror.

So with that, gentle readers, good night. Thank you for reading, and may you all have pleasant dreams.

— Dale Jarvis, Clarke's Beach, May 2017

WORKS REFERENCED

AngelfireRN. Does Death Have a Smell? 26 January 2010. Web accessed 20 November 2016. http://allnurses.com/general-nursing-discussion/does-death-have-452535.html

Beck, Horace. *Folklore of the Sea.* Middletown: Wesleyan University Press, 1973.

Bond, Susan McDonald. *Eric: A Tale of a Red-Tempered Viking.* New York: Grove Press, 1968.

Bown, Addison. Bell Island Ferries of Fomer Years. Web accessed 22 November 2016. https://web.archive.org/web/20120307125735/http://www.bellisland.net/

Burry, Emma. Sunshine Park Killer Urban Legend. Recorded 27 May 2011. Memorial University's Digital Archives Initiative

Chambers, Paul. *Sex and the Paranormal.* London: Blandford Press, 1999.

Coish, Della A., ed. *Tales of Fogo Island.* Fogo Island Literacy Association, 1999.

"Concerning Negro Sorcery in the United States." *Journal of American Folklore* 3.11 (Oct-Dec 1890): 281-287.

"Connor's Webpage on the Vikings in North America." Web

accessed 14 November 2016. http://www.valhalla-lodge.com/quicklinks/conor.html

"Corporal Punishment in England." *Journal of the American Institute of Criminal Law and Criminology* 2.1 (May 1911): 99.

Dahl. Richard S. "Lore of Placentia Bay." *Newfoundland Quarterly* 7.2 (October 1912): 16.

Devine, Maurice A., and Michael J. O'Mara. *Notable events in the history of Newfoundland: six thousand dates of historical and social happenings.* St. John's: Devine & O'Mara, 1900.

Devine, Patrick Kevin (attributed to "P.K.D."). "Father Duffy's Well." *Newfoundland Quarterly* 34.3 (December 1934): 25.

de Vos, Gail. *Tales, rumors, and gossip: Exploring contemporary folk literature in grades* 7-12. Westport: Libraries Unlimited, 1996.

Dohey, Larry. "Cemeteries in St. John's: Archival Moment July 3, 1859." Web accessed 24 November 2016. http://archivalmoments.ca/2016/07/new-cemetery-for-st-johns/

"Editorial." *Decks Awash* 16.3 (May-June 1987): 62.

Eliot, T. S. *Old Possum's Book of Practical Cats* (First American edition). New York: Harcourt, Brace & Co, 1939.

English, L. E. F. "Legends of Newfoundland." *Newfoundland Quarterly* 49.1 (June 1949: 13-16.

English, L.E.F. "Pirate Legends." *Newfoundland Quarterly* 55.4 (December 1956): 34-35.

"Fogo Island—An overview." *Decks Awash* 16.14 (1987): 3-15.

"Folklore of the Port-au-Port Peninsula." 1972. On file, Newfoundland Room, AC Hunter Adult Public Library, St. John's.

Gaulton, Barry C. and Catherine Hawkins. Interim Report: Ferryland (CgAf-02) Permit # 15.20. Web accessed 21 November 2016. https://www.mun.ca/archaeology/people/faculty/bgaulton/Ferryland_Interim_Report_2015.pdf

Georges, Robert A. "The General Concept of Legend: Some Assumptions to be Reexamined and Reassessed." p1-20.

Godwin, Bill, Part 2. Interview with Bill Godwin, Barr'd Islands. Interview conducted by Gerald Pocius and Mark Ferguson, 1989-11-10. Memorial University's Digital Archives Initiative.

"Got Aground." *Evening Telegram* (9 November 1907): 4.

"The Governor and Father Duffy's Well." *Evening Telegram* (20 April 1880): 1.

Hand, Wayland, ed. *American Folk Legend: A Symposium.* Berkeley: U of California Press, 1971.

"Harbor Grace Notes." *Evening Telegram* (27 August 1907): 6.

Hiscock, Philip. "Folklore and Wells." *Downhomer* 12.11 (April 2000): 52-53.

Howley, James P. *The Beothucks or Red Indians: The Aboriginal Inhabitants of Newfoundland.* Cambridge: Cambridge University Press, 1915.

Howley, Michael Francis. "Poor Joe Benoit: A True Story of the West Coast." *Christmas Bells* (1915): 18-19.

"Imperial Parliamentary Delegates Arrive in the City." *Evening Telegram* (1 September 1925): 4.

Jamieson, Charles. "Are there such things as 'Tokens?' Do 'Spirits' Walk Abroad?" *Newfoundland Quarterly* 18.3 (December 1928): 15-16.

James Ryan Diary 1896. Maritime History Archive—James

Ryan Ltd. Diaries, Bonavista. Memorial University's Digital Archives Initiative.

Jarvis, Dale. "Phantom cries from Emily Harbour." *Downhomer* 15.2 (July 2002): 63- 64.

J. D. P. "Legend of Piper's Creek." *Christmas Bells* 10 (December 1901): 6-7.

Kinsella, P. J. "Superstitions of the Outports." *Christmas Bells* 19 (December 1910): 13.

Magnusson, Magnus, ed. *The Vinland Sagas: 'Graenlendinga Saga' and 'Eirik's Saga.'* London: Penguin Books, 1973.

Mansfield, Jack. Jack Mansfield interview, January 3, 1986. Interview conducted by Hiram Silk. Memorial University's Digital Archives Initiative.

Marshall, Ingeborg. *A History and Ethnography of the Beothuk.* Montreal: McGill-Queen's Press, 1998.

Maynard, Lara. "Confronting the Ghost: A Study of Treasure Guardianship in Newfoundland Legends." *Transmission: Culture & Tradition* 1.1 (October 1995): 7-11.

Merrifield, Ralph. *The Archaeology of Ritual and Magic.* London: Guild Publishing, 1987.

Moore, Ruby Andrews. "Superstitions in Georgia." *Journal of American Folklore* 5.18 (Jul-Sep 1892): 230-231.

Morgan, J. "Recollections of Harbour Deep." *Atlantic Guardian* 14.9 (September 1957): 5.

Morris, Don. "Drums at the Graveside; Is Brigus Phantom Real?" *Here In Newfoundland* 1.1 (April 1956): 18.

Nelmes, K, ed. "Archaeology at Ferryland, Newfoundland, 1997." Archaeology in Newfoundland and Labrador 1997. Provincial Archaeology Office. Web accessed 21 November 2016. http://www.btcrd.gov.nl.ca/pao/

arch_in_nl/1997/carter_gaulton_tuck_1997_ferryland.html

Norris, Alicia F. "The Ghost That Went to Sea." *Atlantic Guardian* 2.6 (June 1946): 12-41.

"Obituary Mr. Robert Cole." St. John's *Daily Star*, 1918-12-11.

O'Dea, Brian. *Creepy Canada.* Season 3, Episode 4. OLN (2006).

Opie, Iona and Peter. *The Lore and Language of Schoolchildren.* New York: Oxford University Press, 1959.

"Paddy Casey of Bird Island Cove." NFLD-LAB-L Archives. Web accessed 6 November 2016. http://archiver.rootsweb.ancestry.com/th/read/NFLD-LAB/1998-06/0899177872

Patel, Samir. "From the Trenches: World Roundup." Archaeology 62.5 (September/October 2009). Web accessed 21 November 2016. http://archive.archaeology.org/0909/trenches/world.html

Patterson, George. "Notes on the Folk-Lore of Newfoundland." *Journal of American Folklore* 8 (1 October 1895): 285-290.

"A Phantom Train." *Daily News*, St. John's. 3 April 1907.

Porter, David D. "Discipline in the Navy." *North American Review* 150.401 (April 1890): 409-418.

Primmer, Gwen. "Winter Games and Storytelling of the Inshore Fishery, Fogo Island." *Culture and Tradition* 7 (1983): 17-36.

Raven, David. "'Miracle' cat predicts deaths of 100 people in nursing home." *Mirror* (30 March 2015). Web accessed 5 November 2016. http://www.mirror.co.uk/news/world-news/miracle-cat-predicts-deaths-100-5365056

Rieti, Barbara Gaye. Newfoundland fairy traditions: a study in narrative and belief. A Thesis submitted in partial fulfillment of the requirements for the degree of Doctor of Philosophy, Department of Folklore, Memorial University of Newfoundland, May 1990.

Rollmann, Hans. "The Origin of Fog: A Labrador Inuit Folk Tale." Newfoundland and Labrador Studies 23.1 (2008): 79-84.

Ryan, Don. "Swift Current." *Atlantic Guardian* 14.10 (October 1957): 19-21.

Smith, Paul. *The Book of Nasty Legends.* London: Routledge and Keegan Paul, 1983.

"Special Section: North Harbour to Swift Current." *Decks Awash* 21.6 (November-December 1992): 4-14.

Story, George Morley, ed. *Dictionary of Newfoundland English.* St. John's: Breakwater, 1990.

"Superstitions in Newfoundland." *Journal of American Folklore* 9.34 (July - September 1896): 222-223.

Thomas, Aaron. *The Newfoundland Journal of Aaron Thomas: Able Seaman in H.M.S. Boston.* Ed. Jean M. Murray. London: Longmans, 1968.

Toope, Beatrice and Jesse Cooper, 2. Beatrice Toope and Jesse Cooper interview, July 1, 1969. Interview conducted by Hiram Silk. Memorial University's Digital Archives Initiative.

The Town Crier's Grab-Bag of Newfoundland Folklore. St. Johns: The Town Crier Publishing Co. Ltd., circa 1976.

Tucker, Kathleen. Folklore: *Ghostly Tales, Superstitions and Local Traditions & Customs.* St. Anthony: St. Anthony Basin Resources Inc. Oral History Project, 2014.

Waterman, Jessie. Jessie Waterman interview. Interview conducted by Hiram Silk, date unknown. Memorial University's Digital Archives Initiative.

"Weird Monster Destroys Nets At Grand River." *Western Star* (4 January 1952): 1.

Wells, Julia. Interview with Julia Wells about her life. Interview conducted by Hiram Silk, date unknown. Memorial University's Digital Archives Initiative.

"What Was It?" *Evening Telegram* (28 December 1907): 6.

Whitbourne, Richard. A Discourse and Discovery of Newfoundland, with many reasons to prove how worthy and beneficial a Plantation may there be made, after a far better manner than now it is. Imprinted at London by Felix Kingston, for William Barret, 1620. Web accessed 12 November 2016. https://www.mun.ca/rels/hrollmann/relsoc/texts/whitbourne/whit.html

White, William. "Ghosts and Phantom Lights." *Trinitarian Christmas Number*, December 1925

Widdowson, John. If You Don't Be Good: Verbal Social Control in Newfoundland. Social and Economic Studies No. 21. St. John's: Institute of Social and Economic Research, Memorial University of Newfoundland, 1977.

Wilson, Lisa, ed. *Folk Belief and Legends of Bay Roberts and Area.* St. John's: Heritage Foundation of Newfoundland and Labrador and the Bay Roberts Cultural Foundation Inc., 2014.

Wood, Maureen and Ron Kolek. *A Ghost a Day: 365 True Tales of the Spectral, Supernatural, and Just Plain Scary!* Avon, MA: Adams Media, 2010.

Dale Jarvis works as the Intangible Cultural Heritage Development Officer for the Heritage Foundation of Newfoundland and Labrador, helping communities to safeguard traditional culture, the first full-time provincially funded folklorist position in Canada. Dale holds a B.Sc. in anthropology/archaeology from Trent University, and a M.A. in folklore from Memorial University. He is a past president of the Newfoundland Historic Trust, and has contributed as a board member and volunteer to many local arts and heritage organizations. He regularly teaches workshops on oral history, cultural documentation, folklore project management, and public folklore programming.

By night, Dale is the proprietor of the St. John's Haunted Hike ghost tour and raconteur of local tales. As a storyteller, he performs ghost stories, stories of the fairies and little people, tales of phantom ships and superstitions, and legends and traditional tales from Newfoundland, Labrador, and beyond. His repertoire includes long-form folk and fairy tales from the island, with a wide-ranging knowledge of local legends, tall tales, and myths. A newspaper columnist and author of several books on Newfoundland and Labrador ghost stories and folklore, he is a tireless promoter of local culture.

INDEX

Adams, Ryan 23
Alexander Bay 155, 157, 159
Angle Brook Road, Glovertown 105, 109
Anglo-Newfoundland Development Company 51, 105
Anticosti Island 13
Apsey, George 9
Argentia 69
Ascension Collegiate 23, 79
Avalon Peninsula 158
Avalon Wilderness Preserve 158

Back Cove 150
Bailey, Garland 19
Baine Johnston 21
Balsam Street, St. John's 178
Banks Cove 150
Banks, Jane (Waterman) 150
Banks, John 150
Banks Meadow 150
Banks, William 150
Bareneed xi, 131
Barnes, Daniel R. 123
Barr'd Islands 147
Bay de L'Eau 95, 98
Bay du Nord 139
Bay of Islands 134
Bay Roberts xi, 23, 33, 36, 63, 65, 79, 81, 83, 85, 87, 88, 90, 131, 132, 169
Bay Roberts Cultural Foundation 79, 87, 94
Bay Roberts East 88
Bay St. George 13, 16, 17, 64
Beck, Horace 43
Beaver Pond 169
Belleoram 38
Bell Island 43-45
Bell Island Steamship Company 43
Bennett, C. F. 51

Bennett, Judge 37
Benoit, Joe 13-17
Benoit, Paul 14-16
Beothuk 102, 155-159
Birchy Cove 19, 20
Bird Island Cove 59, 61
Bishop Feild College 83
Bishop's Beach 94
Bishop's Falls 105
Blackbeard 136
Black Duck Siding 119-121
Black Head 45
Blaketown 117
Bloody Bay 158, 159
Bloody Bay Reach 157
Bloody Point 157-159
Bodner, John 116
Bonavista 3, 9, 60, 61, 131, 135, 193, 194
Bonavista Bay 22, 73, 158
Bonavista Peninsula 59, 134
Bond, Susan McDonald 95
Boulevard, St. John's 161-165
Bown, Addison 43
Boyd, Erin 120
Boyd's Cove 49
Bradbury, Robert C. 87
Branch 204
Brenton, Bruce 157
Brigus 9, 66, 83, 86, 87, 169, 171
Brimstone Head 150
Brown's Point 179
Brunvand, Jan 123, 124
Bullen, Josiah 73
Bullen, Meta 73
Burgeo 13, 175
Burin Peninsula 91, 98
Burry, Emma 68
Butt's Point 148
Byrne, Ashley 203

Cabot Tower 129
California 36
Camp Ashanti 119-121, 125
Cann Island 134
Cape Broyle 141
Cape la Hune 33, 38
Cape Pine 21
Cape Shore 135
Cap Rouge 55
Carbonear 23, 25, 45, 116, 118, 187, 189, 193, 202
Carmanville 117, 122
Carroll, Lewis 175
Casey Gulch 59
Casey, Kitty 59-63
Casey, Patrick "Paddy" 59, 61
Catalina 20
Cavendish 30
Chambers, Paul 202
Change Islands 116, 205
Chesapeake, Virgina 136
Chestertown, Maryland 183
Chisel Hill 141
Church Hill, Bay Roberts 65

Church of England 83
Circular Road, St. John's 163
Clarenville 36
Clarke, Eanie 117
Clarke's Beach 77-81, 131, 206
Coish, Della 148, 149, 155
Cokes, E. 71
Colbourne, Winston 102
Cold Brook 117
Cole, Richard 59
Cole, Robert 161
Coles-Hayley, Marilyn 61
Coley's Point xi, xii
Colliers 177, 181, 183
Collins, George 13
Collins, Joseph 13
Colorado River 111
Comfort Cove 177, 180
Comfort Cove Road 180, 181
Conception Bay xi, 9, 11, 85, 87, 93, 131, 137, 183
Conception Harbour 181
Connaigre Peninsula 70
Cook, James 13
Corbett, Brittany 79
Corner Brook 116, 118, 120, 142, 143, 206
Courish, Maggie 130
Crane's Hill, Bay Roberts 88
Crane's Hill Road, Bay Roberts 88
Crewe, Nimshi 59-61
Crouse 55-58
"Crusty Harry" 19
Cupids 131, 183-185
Curley's Cove 159
Custer's Head 158

Dahl, Richard S. 93
Daisy May 57, 58
Davis, Horace 134
Davis, John 134
Dawe, Captain 45
Deadman's Cove 73
Deadman's Cove Road 72
Decker, George 102
Deer Lake 111, 115, 120, 126
Delaney, P. 71
Devine, Patrick Kevin 143, 156
de Vos, Gail 171
d'Iberville, Pierre Le Moyne 157
Doctor's Harbour 33, 38
Dorset, England 137
Dosa, David 26, 27
Dover Castle 91
Dover, England 91
Drummer's Pond 90
Drummer's Rock 87, 89, 90, 94
Duffy, James 139-145
Dunville 90
Duval, Jenelle 118

Eastern Corner, Whiteway 30
Eastport 73
East White Hills Road, St. John's 161
Eiriksfjord, Greenland 97
Eiriksson, Thorstein 96, 97
Eiriksson, Thorvald 96, 97, 102
Eliot, T. S. 188
Elizabeth River 136
Elliston 59, 60, 62
Emily Harbour 7, 9, 11, 12
Empire Avenue, St. John's 163
England 51, 63, 83, 91, 137, 185
English, L. E. F. xi, 133
English, Leo 86
Etheridge's Point 174, 179, 180

Father Duffy's Well 139-145
Feltham, Paula 110
Ferguson, Mark 147
Fermeuse 141
Ferryland 184
Fisher, Chantel 3-6
Fitzgerald, Ned 92
Fleming, Bishop 140
Flynn, Mike 169, 170
Fogo 149, 150
Fogo Island 147-153, 155, 178
Fogo Island Literacy Association 148
Fortune Bay 38, 98
Fox Harbour 90
Fox Island River 119
French's Cove 87, 88
Front Road, Bay Roberts 88, 94
Furlong, Francis 173, 175

Gallows Cove 133
Gander 123
Garden Cove 92
Garia 13, 14, 16
Garia Bay 13, 14
Gaulton, Barry 184
Georges, Robert A. 77
Georgestown, St. John's 189
Georgia 183
Glengarry, Scotland 139
Glovertown 105, 108-111, 113, 159
Godwin, Bill 147, 148
Goose Cove 203
Gosse, Wesley 35
Gough, T. J. 140, 141
Gower Street, St. John's 187, 201
Grand Bank 25, 98
Grand Banks 69
Grand Falls–Windsor 105, 143
Graveyard Cove 11

Gray and Goodland 14
Great Northern Peninsula 55, 103, 115, 121, 203
Green Island 134
Green Point 133
Gulf Stream 69

Hant's Harbour 155, 157, 158
Harbour Breton 69, 72, 73
Harbour Grace 37, 45, 90
Harbour Le Cou 13
Harbour Mille 95, 98, 99
Harmon Air Force Base 115
Hawkins, Catherine 184
Hay Cove 102
Head of Bay D'Espoir 69, 71
Heart's Content 116, 193
Heart's Content Barrens 116
Heart's Delight 31, 195
Hedderson, Jack 102
Heritage New Perlican 205
Heritage Walking Trail 94
Hermitage 197
Hicks, Lloyd 60
Higgins, W. J. 143
Hiscock, Philip 139
Holyrood 140, 142
Hoover Dam 111
Hopkins, Anastacia 119
Howley, James P. 157-159
Howley, Michael Francis 14, 16, 17
Howse, Matthew 119
Huntley, Dick 92
Hussey, Greta 133

Iceland 97, 100, 101
Igloo Road 117, 122
Indian Burying Place 127
Indian Cove 93
Indian Head 64
Ingonish, Nova Scotia 136
Ingstad, Anne (Stine) 95, 101
Ingstad, Helge 95, 101
Ireland 136, 140, 142, 189
Ireland's Eye 42, 46, 136, 137
Island Harbour 148, 149
Islington 29, 32

Jamieson, Charles 1
J. Munn and Company 9
Joe Batt's Arm 173, 174, 177-179
John Guy 43
Jones, George 66
Juggler's Cove 132
Junction Brook 111
J.W. Hiscock's 9

Keeping, Jeff 116
Kelly's Brook 93
King Academy 72
King's Bridge 161

King's Bridge Road, St. John's 161, 165
Kinsella, P. J. 81
Kipawa 43
Knights of Columbus 145
Kolek, Ron 100

Labrador Current 69
Labrador Straits 7
Lajeunesse, Henri 55, 57, 58
Lambert, Ryan 72, 73
Lane, Watson 159
L'Anse aux Meadows 95, 98-101, 103
La Poile 13, 25
Larkin's Hill 91
Lewisporte 116, 180
Little Bay West 73
Livingstone Street, St. John's 178
Loch Oich 139
London, England 63
Long Harry 131
Long Range Mountains 14
Loyal Orange Lodge 99

Mad Rock 132, 133
Main Dam 111
Manila Film Centre 111
Mansfield, Jack 51-53
Marshall, Christa 33, 34
Marshall, Ingeborg 158, 159
Martin, Albert 70, 71
Mary 43-45
Marystown 33
Marysvale 83, 85
Masters, Pauline (Chislett) 29-31
Matthews, Eileen (Balsom) 205
Mattis Point 63-65
Mattis Point Hill 64
Maynard, Lara 134
McKay, Smith 51
Memorial University of Newfoundland 36, 70, 116, 124, 140
Michelin, Sean 116
Mi'kmaq 14, 25, 33, 139
Miller, Leone (Etheridge) 173
Miller's Passage 72
Minty, William 60
Mississippi River Bridge 111
Money Point 131, 136, 137
Montreal, Quebec 142
Moore, Ruby (Andrews) 183
Moores, Alice 7, 8
Mooring Cove 197
Morgan, J. 167
Morris, Don 86
Motion Head 134
Mount Carmel Cemetery 161, 164
Mount Pearl 63

Muddy Cove 95, 101, 103
Mullock, John Thomas 162
Murphy, Alice (McGrath) 181
Murray, Patrick 155, 156
Musgrave Harbour 131, 134

Nain 9, 69
Newfoundland Constabulary 162
Newfoundland Museum 86
New Glasgow, Nova Scotia 37
Newman's Cove 22
New Perlican 155, 157, 184, 205
Niagara, Ontario 142
Nolan, Rebekah 36
Noordhof, Gina 101, 102
Norris, Alicia 55-58
Norris Dam 111
Norseman Restaurant 101
Norstead Viking Village 95
North River 78, 79
Norway 21
Noseworthy, Angela 125
Notre Dame Bay 51, 205
Nova Scotia 37, 117, 136

Old Hag 65, 197-206
Opie, Iona 36
Opie, Peter 36
Otterbury 131

Paradise 203
Parks Canada 95, 106
Parsons, Travis George 25, 26
Pasadena 118-120, 125
Pass Island 197
Patterson, George 37
Payne, Dee 195
Payne's Harbour 148
Pearl, Anne 63
Pearl, James 63
Pearson, Cindy 164, 165
Penney, Daniel 189-191
Penton, Barry 150
Penton, Dean 178-180
Petty Harbour 135
Philadelphia 181
Philippines 111
Pike, Lloyd 197-199
Pilley's Island 51-53
Piper's Creek 92
Piper's Hole 91, 93
Piper's Hole River 91
Placentia 90, 91, 143
Placentia Bay 93, 158
Pocius, Gerald 147
Pollux 21
Port au Port Peninsula 64
Port de Grave 131, 133
Porter, David D. 89
Porter, Tom 60
Portugal Cove 140
Port Union 3, 4
Powell, Ambrose 7

Power, Bride 85
Power, Tony 204
Primmer, Isaac 147
Prince Edward Island 200
Progress 44

Quebec 43, 133
Queens Road, St. John's 178
Quidi Vidi 162
Quidi Vidi Lake 161, 163
Quinn, Molly (Murphy) 181, 182

Rattling Brook 92
Reardon's Rock 155
Red Bay 7, 133
Red Indian Lake 155, 158
Rencontre East 38
Reykjavik, Iceland 100
Rhode Island 26, 27
Rideout, Kate 180, 181
Rieti, Barbara 140
Riverhead 66, 140
Riverside Road, Glovertown 111
Roach, Emmie May (Crane) 88
Roach, Harry 88
Roach, Sandra 87, 89, 90, 94
Robbins, Debbie 117, 122
Roberts, Paula 36
Rollmann, Hans 70
Rome, Italy 97
Rorke 9
Royal Canadian Mounted Police (RCMP) 123
Royal Navy 92
Russell, Josh 79, 80
Ryan, Daniel A. 9
Ryan, Don 91
Ryan, Edmund "Ned" 20
Ryan, James 9
Ryan, Shirley 19-22

St. Andrew's Church 150
St. Anthony 203
St. Anthony Basin Resources Inc. 101
Sainte Marie 55
St. George's 14, 17
St. John's 3, 27, 43-46, 59, 61, 68, 98, 133, 140, 143, 157, 161, 163, 177, 178, 187, 189, 195, 201
St. Malo 55, 56
St. Mary's 140, 142
Salmonier 141, 143
Salmonier Line 139, 145
Samms, Kharis 126, 127
Sandy Cove 59, 61, 62, 69, 73, 75, 155, 156
Sandy Point 14
San Luis Obispo, California 36
Saunders, David 106
Scotland 139
Scouts Canada 125
Second Field, Fogo 150

Shakespeare, William 156
Shamrock 9
Ship Cove Pond 133
Shoal Bay 131, 135, 137
Shoal Cove 72
Short Beach xi
Sidney, Ohio 111
Signal Hill, St. John's 129, 130, 133
Silk, Hiram 42, 46, 150
Silver Birches Cub Camp 119
Skiffington, Leonard 20, 22
Slaney-Miller, Cindy 193, 194
Smith, Paul 124
Smokey 9
Somerton, Megan 201
Sound Island 158
Southern Cross 19-23
South River 33, 36, 131
Southside Road, St. John's 191
Southwest Arm 47
Spaniard's Bay 23-25, 33, 35, 169, 171
Sparkes, Audrey 87
Stephenville 115, 117, 119, 120, 122
Stewart, Rod 105-113
Street, Angela 116
Strickland, Olive 132, 133
Stroud, Harold 159
Sugar Loaf 45
Sullivan, Dave 115
Sullivan, Tom 59
Sunshine Park 67, 68
Swift Current 83, 91

Tar Barrel 9
Taylor, Alan 125
Taylor, Freeman 134
Taylor, Mamie 100
Taylor's Hill 52
Tennessee 111
Terra Nova National Park 106
Terra Nova River 109
Terra Nova Sulphite Company 105
Thomas, Aaron 69
Tilley Farm Road 61
Tilt Cove 51, 126, 127
Tilting 155
Toope, Beatrice 42, 46
Torbay 66, 131, 133, 134
Toronto, Ontario 142
Tors Cove 69, 71
Tracey Hill, Red Bay 133
Trinity 19, 43, 46
Trinity Bay 19, 29, 43, 46, 136, 137
Trinity Historical Society 19
Tuck, Dwayne 157
Tucker, Grant 157, 158
Tucker, Kathleen 101, 102
Turk's Gut 85, 86

Turk's Gut Heritage Committee 85
Turk's Gut Heritage House 85, 86
Turpin, Michael 155, 156
Turpin's Rock 156

UNESCO World Heritage Site 95
United States Navy 89
University of Alberta 171
University of Kansas 123
Upper Island Cove 23

Valhalla Lodge 101
Vikings 95, 101-103
Vinegar Hill, Clarke's Beach 131, 133

Wales 36
Wall, Krista 203
Waterman, Jessie 49, 50
Water Street, Harbour Grace 65
Well of the Seven Heads 139
Wells, Doug 72
Wells, Julia 150
Welsh, Kimberley 79
Wesley Gosse Memorial Building 24
West Haven Camp 125, 126
Whalen, Rhonda 164
Whiteway 30
White, William 19
W. I. Bishop 111
Wilson, Lisa 23, 79, 87, 131-133
Wilsonville Avenue, Clarke's Beach 77, 79
Wilson, W. 158
Wiltshire, Ezra 5
Wiltshire, Wesley 4
Winsor, George 51
Winsor, Mary 51
Wood, Maureen 100

ALSO BY DALE JARVIS

Haunted Waters
ISBN: 9781897317792

From an encounter with a shrieking horror on Signal Hill, St. John's, to the legend of the headless pirate of Red Bay, Labrador, folklorist Dale Jarvis conjures up stories of white horses, men in black, haunted punts, vanishing boats, and things that go bump in the basement.

With its tales of premonitions of death, eerie phantoms, and strange creatures, Newfoundland and Labrador is truly a haunted place. Beware, gentle reader! The unquiet spirits of dogs, wolves, little girls, ships, and soldiers drift through these pages. You may even run into the Old Hag herself, Newfoundland and Labrador's most infamous nighttime visitor.

Blending local history, folklore, eyewitness interviews, and archival research, *Haunted Waters* is the latest collection of ghostly tales from one of Canada's finest, and creepiest, storytellers.

WWW.FLANKERPRESS.COM

ALSO BY DALE JARVIS

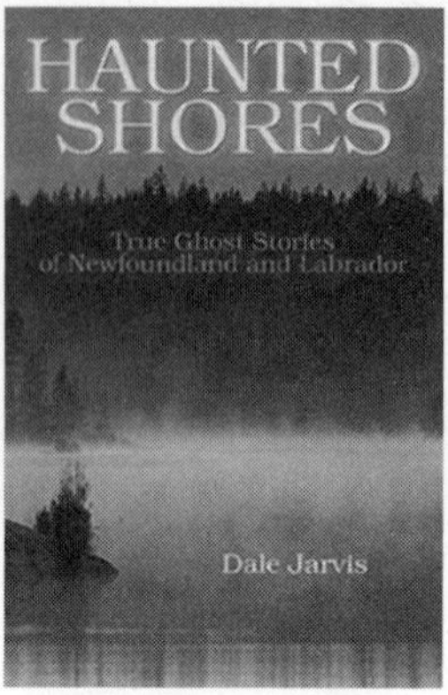

Haunted Shores

ISBN: 9781894463546

The province of Newfoundland and Labrador is rich with tales of ghost ships, mysterious lights, sinister spectres, tokens of impending death, headless pirates and murdered loves. *Haunted Shores: True Ghost Stories of Newfoundland and Labrador* is an eerie exploration of the phantom-filled nooks and crannies of the province. Why does a mournful lady ghost return to Arnold's Cove every November? Do ghostly submarines still sail the waters of Trinity Bay? What is the most haunted street in St. John's?

Drawn from both archival sources and first-hand accounts, the stories herein weave together anecdote, oral tradition, history and folklore to form a rich tapestry depicting a rarely explored side of Newfoundland and Labrador.

Read the book, if you dare . . .